PRIMER
OF
PRAYER

by
Rev. Bartholomew J. O'Brien

Edited and Published by
FAITH PUBLISHING COMPANY
P.O. Box 237
Milford, Ohio 45150

Published by Faith Publishing Company

Scriptural Text: Contraternity of Christian Doctrine
                Copyright © 1970, (New American bible)

Copyright © 1991, Faith Publishing Company

Library of Congress Catalog Card No.: 91-071541

ISBN: 0-9625975-8-9

Table of Contents

Dedication

To the Blessed Virgin Mary, our dear
Mother, who, with Saint Joseph, made
the time to teach her divine Son, and to
share with Jesus, the prayers of their
time... and to my dear Parents who also
made the time to teach me and to share
with me the prayers of our time.

Introduction

This treatise on prayer is only an introduction to prayer. It is a primer meant for beginners. It points out the way to pray and the growth in prayer with the hope that the reader will continue the way and the growth by means of the splendid volumes that have been well written on all the subjects introduced on these pages. It is further hoped that many will develop an enthusiasm for prayer and that the treatise will inspire them to follow and pursue the way, and live out the way, and grow in prayer for the remainder of their lives. I like to think of this small primer as the tiny seed from which the mighty oak of prayer will grow.

This treatise opens by simply recalling the prayer that everyone knows, the prayer of the lips, vocal prayer, which happily claims as its own the traditional *Our Father* and *Hail Mary*.

Only after the reader becomes comfortable with the opening pages of this primer is the definition of prayer brought forth.

The readers whom I had in mind while writing consist of some of my friends and relatives who are truly wonderful people, well educated, successful in many ways, prayerful and religious, but who seem to be limited in their prayer life to vocal prayers, and vocal prayers alone. This is no tragedy or mistake or error; it is merely a fact. Because I love these people, it is my sincere desire to help them to experience more, to grow stronger in the life of prayer, to be introduced to the rich tradition of prayer which received its beginning when Jesus taught His Apostles His own composition in honor of His Father and our Father.

In my sincere efforts to be simple and clear, perhaps on occasion my style of writing has become over-simplified. At times, there are repetitions for the sake of better emphasis and understanding. Possibly a few introductions are too abbreviated. In the spirit of enthusiasm, sometimes a balance was difficult to reach. May the message speak louder than my style of writing!

In my zeal to introduce the various forms of prayer which truly mean so very much to me personally, maybe I also have failed to inspire the love which I so sincerely wish others to experience in prayer. As a rule or in general, time for praying should be a time for joy, happiness and fulfillment. Prayer time is the important time when we meet God with all His love, kindness and goodness. It should be a positive experience and spirit-filled encounter. Such a spirit has moved me in writing, from page to page, from beginning to end.

These words of Jesus mean so very much to me: *"Your hearts will be full of joy and that joy no one will take from you. . .Your joy will be complete."* (*John* 16:22, 24). As you read this treatise, and as you try to practice what it teaches, may the Holy Spirit so touch you and move you and that YOUR JOY WILL BE COMPLETE.

PRIMER
OF
PRAYER

Chapter 1

Morning and Night Prayers

Morning and night prayers will remain a very important tradition in the lives of many people. Even though the lives of these individuals are crowded by adverse conditions which obscure the loving fatherhood of God, nevertheless, some effort (and at times, heroic effort) is made and some "thing" is attempted by them to fulfill what is commonly referred to as morning prayers and night prayers.

For example, a simple Sign of the Cross constitutes morning prayer; for others, perhaps the recitation of the morning offering (while hurrying off to work) fulfills the tradition of morning prayer. Yet, there are many (maybe more than we think) who kneel in reverence and pray, with hands folded, the traditional formulas once prayed every morning in the parish school. The fact remains that, in spite of the frantic activities of a tension-filled world, daily prayers are still offered to God in some form, some shape, and in some manner, morning after morning and night after night.

How did the habit of reciting daily prayers enter into the lives of such a large percentage of the people? Probably most of us could say, with happy memories, "My mother taught me," or "My father trained me." Perhaps after the morning alarm went off, one of our parents ever reminded us: ". . .and don't forget to say your prayers!" And perhaps after the good night kiss, one of our parents always added: ". . .and don't forget to say your prayers!" There was usually a reminder given in most

1

homes, but probably without a great amount of supervision. It is difficult to evaluate the quality and the quantity of the daily prayers program as it evolved from childhood into adulthood...and as it stands today in these later years of life.

I shall ever be most thankful to my mother who taught me, from my tenderest years, prayer after prayer. She knew that my memory was capable of storing a multitude of prayers for the present and for the years to come. She realized that the memory of a child is like a massive, strong, empty building waiting to receive and to store volumes of special memories like prayers. Time can never erase these volumes of special memories, because they are carefully put away when the memory building is new and fresh and open and ready to receive them and to preserve them with care and with enthusiasm. And so today I am in possession of a repertoire of prayers, the meaning of which now becomes more realistic with the accumulation of experiences and years.

My father taught me, not by storing my memory with formulas, but by storing my memory with his good example of praying, especially of praying his morning prayers. My father was a farmer. He got up early, dressed, and then awakened me. When I joined him in the kitchen (the warmest room in the farm house) he was always kneeling by the kitchen stove in prayer. I never disturbed him. Rheumatism or no rheumatism; arthritis or no arthritis, he followed the tradition of getting down on his two knees and remaining for ten minutes or more in prayer. What prayers he offered, I do not know. I never asked him. At the time, I took his manner of praying for granted. I just thought that this is the way a man prayed. I took for granted that everyone prayed this way. Therefore, his way was my way. And so I followed his way. It was that simple. And the memory is with me to this day. I still pray like my father, on my knees. The power of his example continues to influence my prayer life, even today some forty years after his death. That is the way it was with my dad: first he prayed and then he went to the barn to care for the cows and the other animals...and I followed behind to help out as best I could. But I'll always remember...

Parents are blessed in being the very first ones to have the honor of helping to pass the faith on to their children. It is an honor no parent should ever delegate totally or lightly to anyone else. I recall having a telephone conversation with a mother who was most anxious to enroll her daughter in the parish school so that "the Sisters could teach my little girl her prayers." As patiently as possible, I explained that the honor of passing on the faith was a gift given primarily to her, the mother, and to her husband, and should never be handed completely over to another, even to a dedicated Sister. The teachers in the parish school gladly cooperate with the parents and reinforce the teaching the child received at home. God made the home before He made the school; God also created parents before He created teachers. Or better, maybe God created them all in one, and it was **time** that brought about a division. It is best that all work together as a team for God's glory.

If we go searching beyond the parents into the centuries gone by, we find the origin of morning prayers and evening prayers in the daily prayers of the monks in the monasteries and the cloistered nuns in the convents. The people desired to imitate the religious. They followed their good example. Many of the common folks could not read; Latin was not the language of every day life. But they could see and understand and be edified by the daily example of the monks and nuns and gradually, the people on the farms and in the villages began to imitate them. The religious up on the hills sang their Gregorian Chants in praise of the Lord, and the simple laity down in the valleys prayed their *Pater's* and *Ave's,* also in praise of the Lord.

Although Jesus had only three years in which to fulfill His life's mission, He never neglected to make time in which to pray to His Father. The monks, nuns, and lay folk ever tried to follow His powerful example. Scripture tells us that *"he would always go off to some place where he could be alone and pray."* (*Luke* 5:16). There were times when His night prayer continued into the morning. That is, Jesus spent the night in prayer to His Father.

Saint Luke writes that Jesus *"went out into the hills to pray;
and he spent the whole night in prayer to God."* (*Luke* 6:12).

It is very clear from Sacred Scripture that Jesus did pray. Saint
Luke makes it very evident that Jesus took time from His busy,
active schedule to pray. But how did He pray? What did He
say? Did the Father pray back to Him? Did Jesus make use of
the one hundred and fifty Psalms? Did Jesus know them by heart?
Was it possible that Jesus possessed a manuscript of some kind?
Was a manuscript necessary? When did He sleep if He spent
the whole night in prayer? Was He alone? Did the apostles follow His example? How can we follow His example? What can
we do to be more like Christ? How can we imitate Him in prayer?

Over the centuries, followers of Jesus have imitated Him in a
simple, humble way, through the custom of praying daily the
morning and night prayers. There are no answers to the many
questions concerning Jesus at prayer. Perhaps the nearest we can
come to an answer as to how Jesus prayed, is to turn to the
Gospel of Saint John and to read chapter seventeen. On the night
before His execution, Jesus spent the hours following the final
supper, with His closest friends, the Apostles. He opened up
His Sacred Heart and gave the divine force of His love free play
to pour out the powerful message of love which He came to
planet earth to reveal. This message of love is found in chapters
13, 14, 15 and 16 (the teenage chapters) of the Gospel according
to Saint John. Then, as the night grew later and He awaited the
coming of Judas, His love was directed to His Father. For Jesus,
night time was a convenient prayer time. Usually at night He
was alone. But this last night before His crucifixion, He was
with the eleven. Jesus seemed to pass naturally into the state
of contemplation, and as a silent presence pervaded the upper
room, Jesus addressed His Father. His beloved disciple, John,
with his keen youthful memory, recorded that prayer, and Divine
Providence preserved that recording for us in the famous chapter seventeen.

How did Jesus pray? Read that chapter. And remaining in the
glorious presence of His Father, Jesus continued His prayer in

the garden, where He experienced the suffering side of infinite love. Then, Judas arrived . . .

The prayers which are known as morning and night prayers are usually classified under **"vocal prayer."** There are as many kinds or ways of praying as there are kinds or ways of preaching or teaching or singing. For example, there is meditative praying, contemplative praying, and many others as well. "Vocal prayer" is just one of many. It is the most common. There are some who look upon vocal prayer as the only method of praying. Others hold the opinion that if there are other kinds of prayers (that is, other ways of praying) those are for the theologians and for those in monasteries and convents. Most people start with and continue with vocal prayer. But all the various methods of praying are for everyone.

Nevertheless, a person can become a great saint with vocal prayer alone. In later chapters, we shall be introduced to some of the other methods of praying. Maybe God will invite us to follow other kinds of prayer; maybe we shall be attracted to other ways of praying and become more comfortable praying with other methods apart from vocal prayer.

Without doubt, the Holy Sacrifice of the Mass is the most sublime and dignified of all types of vocal prayer. In fact, the Mass is more than just vocal prayer. The Mass is our central act of worship. The same Jesus, who offered Himself in a bloody manner on Calvary, is present and is offered in an unbloody manner at the altar.

The Rosary is an extremely popular form of vocal prayer and should be greatly encouraged. Among the many other examples there are the litanies, novena prayers, traditional prayers, plus the endless number of prayers found in the popular prayer books and in the Bible.

Of all the prayers or formulas composed for vocal prayer, the most popular (as everyone knows) is that composed by Christ Himself, and given to us by Him for the glory of His Father and as a model for all future formulas, namely, the *Lord's Prayer:*

Our Father, who art in heaven,
1) *hallowed be thy name;*
2) *thy kingdom come;*
3) *thy will be done on earth as it is in heaven.*
4) *Give us this day our daily bread;*
5) *and forgive us our trespasses as we forgive those who trespass against us;*
6) *and lead us not into temptation,*
7) *but deliver us from evil.*
Amen.

The longer ending which is very popular among many Christians, *"For thine is the kingdom, and the power, and the glory, now and forever,"* was a later addition to the Lord's Prayer. It is called a doxology or liturgical ending. A doxology (together with the Amens) was often added to prayers in the early Church. However, the words of this doxology are not found in the original Scriptures of the Bible. That is why tradition has not associated this ending with the popular recitation of the Our Father.

After Vatican II, the Church added the doxology to the revised Liturgy of the Mass without attaching the words directly to the conclusion of the Our Father. The words (with a slight modification) now read in the English translation: *"For the kingdom, the power and the glory are yours, now and forever!"*

Because the phrase has been honored for centuries in the Church, it was not set aside by the Church. Rather, it was given a most distinctive and truly proper placing in the Liturgy, but it has not been popularized in the praying of the Lord's Prayer.

Chapter 2

Vocal Prayer

Probably eighty percent of those who pray use **vocal prayer** and only vocal prayer. From time to time, under certain circumstances, they may drift (or be inspired) into other forms of praying but they may not recognize that what they are doing is truly praying. They may refer to the occasion as a distraction, or merely day dreaming, or wasting time, or just drowsing off. They may recall the occasion as unworthy of mentioning to anyone. They may even feel ashamed of themselves. Besides, maybe they never discuss, or even bring up the subject of prayer. They hold that prayer is too personal a subject for sharing or casual conversation. After all, who is interested in my distractions! Not having a spiritual director, close friend, or an understanding spouse or a confessor, to whom does one go to talk over one's "day dreams"?

It must be stressed that being tied down to only vocal prayers is not always an impediment to spiritual growth. Saint Teresa writes in her *Interior Castle* (Peers, Vol. II, p. 246), that there is room in convents for people of all kinds, and that vocal prayer will bring a person as much benefit and merit as would have been obtained in other ways, and perhaps more. Saint Teresa adds that a life of only vocal prayer can be a "great mortification."

Perhaps that explains why so many people find prayer very difficult. Such prayer, day in and day out, can become monotonous, very dry, almost meaningless, and especially devoid of any experience of God's presence. Yet, let it ever be kept in mind that there are exceptions, and let us ever be thankful to God for His infinite kindness to those who persevere in the practice of vocal prayer.

The conclusion nevertheless is that many well-meaning people adhere to vocal prayers. Maybe they have a fear of change. Perhaps if they wish to change, to whom do they go, or what do they read, or how do they bring about a change? I shall attempt to address these questions in a later portion of this book.

Here and now, I hope it will be helpful to examine some suggestions and to create some conditions that will assist those individuals to become better vehicles for God's love during their daily routine of praying vocally.

Here are seven points focused on brightening up the recitation of one's daily vocal prayers, that is, on bringing the Holy Spirit more forcefully into vocal prayer.

1. He loves me!

Whoever you are reading this account on prayer, please say over and over again (maybe one hundred times) the words: "God loves ME!" God loves you and He has put this particular writing about prayer into your pathway, and has invited you to pick it up and to read it...at least a part of it...God is extending an invitation to you: **Read it!** What the invitation will develop into may become clearer later on. God has placed an interest in prayer within you; you did not put it there yourself.

That interest is a second invitation! Do not call it a mere *happening*. In simple, quiet ways, God is inviting you into friendship with Him. This is still another invitation! No mere *coincidence!* Whether this written account on prayer is good or bad is not important. What is important is that God is using it as a way of making His will known to you right now, whoever you are. In brief, God is inviting you personally to read about prayer, to develop an interest in prayer, and to grow in friendship through prayer, with Him Who loves you.

Probably the one message God is giving to you is simply: "I

love YOU!" God is saying to you that He wants you to be aware of His love for you, His very personal love for you. He knows your name, your address, your age, your dreams, your temptations, your telephone number, your thoughts last evening at 9:27 o'clock, your everything, and He still is saying to you: "I love YOU!" If you can say one hundred times, more or less, "God loves ME!"—you will soon begin to believe it...even to experience it. God will give you the power (or the grace) to believe it. God will give you the power (or the grace) to believe it. If you believe it, then your daily prayers addressed to Someone who loves YOU will take on a fresh, new, enthusiastic experience. You are developing a friendship.

Friendship has warmth and love. Daily vocal prayers wrapped up in warmth and love are a new creation. All this and more can come forth from those simple words of friendship: "God loves ME!" And maybe the time will come when Jesus, because of your friendship, will begin to "pray to you."

As I write down these thoughts, there is a plaque on the wall in front of me which reads so very appropriately for this one moment:

> A friend is someone
> who knows all about you...
> but...
> likes you
> anyway.   (That's God!)

2. To talk and to listen!

Everyone needs someone with whom they can talk about their prayer life, or even about their lack of prayer life. Although we are living today in a world where the rise of tension parallels the rise of technology, nevertheless, we are also living in a world where prayer is an accepted subject of conversation. "Could we talk about prayer for a little while?" or "May I speak to you about prayer while we are traveling on our way?" or "Are you interested in prayer?" or "That reminds me of a workshop I attended recently on prayer. Would you be interested?" Those questions are not out of place in our world which is racing toward the second millennium. Broach the subject. Have no fear. Take a risk. It may unlock new worlds.

In the past, a priest was always "my confessor and spiritual director." That still holds. However, today God has blessed us with very capable sisters, nuns, brothers, and lay persons who cannot serve as confessors, but who can serve as spiritual directors or listeners, conversationalists with whom we may wish to have a casual chat in order to clarify our thinking. Priests of course, fit into the same category. We may not wish this priest to be our confessor, but we may wish him to listen to us and share with us, perhaps formally in the rectory office, or informally over lunch.

There are others too who can serve as someone who will listen. Blessed is that married person who has a spouse who will listen. Blessed too is the person who has a friend, neighbor, or relative who will listen. In brief, blessed is the person who has access to a listening ear. Even one is better than none. We all have acquaintances who have talking lips, but we have few who have listening ears, and who will lend those listening ears to us for just a while, maybe for the space of leisurely drinking a cup of coffee.

I recall being called to the rectory office where I found a middle-aged man in great distress. He did not even give me time to greet him, stranger that he was, but began his tragic story immediately. He talked out his heart, soul, body, mind, emotions, and all. I lent him my listening ears. He had to get what was inside, outside. He needed to objectify (that is, to put into some order) the confusion that was going on within him. As he talked and talked, things were falling into some kind of order; he was gradually experiencing a healing. He grasped the answer he needed and then jumped to his feet, shook my hand with enthusiasm, and praised my kindness for taking the time to assist a brother in need. He dashed out of the office in jubilation, saying in a loud, happy voice: "Thank you, Father. We sure need more understanding priests like You!" And I had said nothing!

3. Be Consistent!

If your prayer life consists mainly in morning prayers or in evening prayers, it is prudent and helpful to have a definite list of those vocal prayers. It is not always worthy of God for us to leave our daily prayers up to the mood in which we find ourselves at prayer time, or to the circumstances in which we are placed. We have a duty to pray; let us therefore fulfill our duty. . .and fulfill it well. A sincere person fulfills her or his duty regardless of the up's and down's of daily life. If a person has seven morning prayers, then that person prays seven; if the person has six evening prayers, then the person prays six. We must not permit ourselves to become scrupulous, but we need to discipline ourselves to become dutiful. Surely the time will someday come when definite vocal formulas will give way to spontaneous acts of love. Discipline will give way to friendship, that is, to love. Not that vocal formulas will give way entirely, but spontaneous prayer will become more rewarding. In Heaven there is no discipline; in Heaven, there is only love. . .Discipline gives way to love.

In the business world, records are kept. Workers are then rewarded for good records. Promotions are granted and vacations are merited because of the good records. God is not a record keeper. But when we are tempted to become careless, let us ever remember that God will not be outdone in generosity.

4. Variety helps!

Variety is an important item in our lives. God has taught us that lesson through the variety of the seasons, and the variety of the weather. Variety is important even in our prayer life. It is wise to evaluate our daily prayers. Are we satisfied with them? Should we change the arrangement of our daily prayers? Would it be wise to eliminate this prayer and to add another? Has familiarity brought on carelessness, or monotony, or humdrum attitudes?

It is possible to recite a series of prayers and to come to the final prayer without realizing a single thought or inspiration.

That may not be sinful, or even an act of carelessness, but we are forced to admit that such a recitation is less worthy of God.

Does a prayer offered without realizing a single thought or inspiration ever reach the Throne of God in Heaven? Does God accept every prayer, good or bad? Do the angels, as God's messengers, carry every prayer, whether it is good or bad or indifferent, to the Throne of God? Are prayers recited carelessly ever segregated? Does God listen to the words of a prayer or does God measure the love with which a prayer is recited? Does God grow tired of the same prayers? Does God grow tired of the love that gives life to prayers? Ask God to answer these questions for you. Listen for the answers. God has all the answers.

Common sense tells us that we should at least either change the sequence of our prayers or substitute other prayers as a way of adding new vitality to our daily tribute to God. Periodically, such an evaluation should be made, perhaps on Ash Wednesday, or during the days preceeding the New Year, or during one's annual retreat. If prayers are recited in this sequence:

$$1 - 2 - 3 - 4 - 5 - 6 - 7$$

it is suggested that the sequence be changed to:

$$7 - 6 - 5 - 4 - 3 - 2 - 1$$

or to:

$$7 - 5 - 3 - 1 - 6 - 4 - 2$$

The secret is variety. We are human and variety helps to keep us alert. Perhaps during March, we might substitute the litany of Saint Joseph; during May, the litany of Our Lady; and during June, that of the Sacred Heart. Variety!

In the "Divine Office" or the "Liturgy of the Hours" which is the daily prayer book for priests, sisters, nuns, brothers (and many lay persons), there are 365 varieties, one for each day.

No two days are exactly the same. The Church wisely knows the weaknesses that are developed through monotony.

In following the practical example of the Church in promoting variety, it is recommended that some different prayers be substituted for, not added to, the present list of morning and evening vocal prayers. The substitution would keep the numerical listing of prayers the same. Perhaps the substitutions could center around seasonal prayers. For example, a Lenten prayer honoring Jesus on Calvary could be discontinued for an Easter prayer honoring the Resurrected Jesus. In brief, variety is one of the secrets which helps us to pray our morning and evening prayers with "attention, reverence, and devotion."

While we are on the subject of variety in prayer, I wish to tell a little story (it is only just a fantasy), about a saint who asked Jesus to do a special favor for a desperate individual on earth. Jesus most kindly performed a miracle immediately, but the saint was given the credit. The individual on earth immediately promised daily to offer the saint's prayer in thanksgiving until death. After fifty-two years of listening to this one prayer, repeated night after night, faster and faster over the years, the saint finally pleaded with God:

> "Dear Lord, please inspire my client to discontinue bothering me night after night with that so-called prayer. I refuse to listen to it any longer. While I appreciate the spirit of thanksgiving, the prayer in no way honors me; in fact, I feel dishonored each time it sounds in my ears."

With much graciousness, God answered the request. (The lesson is quite obvious.) Do not be afraid to discontinue a prayer. Do not be superstitious! If you experience a desire or a need to discontinue a prayer, such a desire or need probably comes with love from the prudent heart of the Lord Himself.

Before the recitation of daily prayers, the following prayer (a portion of which was just quoted) is sincerely recommended.

The prayer is adapted from the prayer given before the recitation of the "Liturgy of the Hours."

> "Lord, open my lips to praise your Holy Name. Cleanse my heart of any worthless, evil, or distracting thoughts. Give me the wisdom and love necessary to pray with ATTENTION, REVERENCE, and DEVOTION. Father, let my prayer be heard in your presence, for it is offered through Christ our Lord. Amen."

5. Where to Pray!

How many pictures have been painted of little children kneeling reverently (and sometimes not so reverently), at their beds saying their good-night prayer before jumping under the covers! Over the years, the bed has become the "prie-dieu" or kneeler for prayer. Of late, the place of prayer has been forced into the car, the office, or the snack bar during the coffee break. God is not as fussy about the place of prayer as He is about our mind (with its endless distractions) and our heart (with its restless emotions). The conclusion is this: in today's world, where technology and production are growing wild, everyone needs to discover the place that is most congenial for her or him. God is everywhere; God will find you and listen to you regardless of where you are.

However, there must be some way by which a quiet nook or corner can be located, and where silence and peace can be quickly created for prayer. Maybe in the blue prints of future homes, architects will find an oversize closet where they will point out to their clients: ". . .and this is the prayer room. . .and if you ever sell, and your buyer is not interested in a prayer room, it can easily be converted into a sewing room, a den, a store room for odds and ends, or a small business office at home."

Even in the houses already built, creative minds can find a corner where something can be added or changed and made into a prayer room.

There are always other possibilities such as stopping at the parish church, parking in the silent area of the local park, sitting in the backyard swing, or even setting aside a silent period (maybe 7:00 to 8:30 p.m.) by having a daily curfew within the home. Blessed is the home where one can daily listen to at least one hour of silence!

There is a very simple conclusion and it is this: where there is a will, there is a way. And too, when all is said and done, out of all the suggestions, maybe the bedroom still remains the best room for praying, and the bed itself the best prie-dieu for kneeling.

6. In Bed?

Surely after reading this far, fifty-eight percent of the readers of these pages are saying quietly and with satisfaction to themselves: "But space for praying is no problem for me. I just pray in bed and then fall off to sleep. My prayers help me to fall quickly to sleep. It is all so simple!"

An immediate reply to this tradition of reciting our official morning and night prayers in bed is: "Let us offer our official prayers to God in an official way. But let us offer our casual words of love to God in the spirit of the Psalmist who signs:

On my bed I remember you.
On you I muse through the night. (Psalm 63).

Where to pray is not a question of sin. Nor is it a question of right and wrong. It is a question of how do we best approach the Almighty God! Daniel in his canticle sang out:

Praise the Lord, all you works of the Lord. Praise
and exalt him above all forever. Angels of the Lord,
bless the Lord. You heavens, bless the Lord. (Daniel 3).

Everyone must answer the question for herself or himself: "How can I best praise the Lord and exalt the Lord and bless the Lord?" Surely our Father in Heaven will graciously accept the guidance and the decision of one's own conscience.

There is another question closely associated with the previous question about praying one's regular prayers in bed. Must I pray my daily prayers on my knees? To pray on one's knees is a very traditional way of praying. It is a symbol of humility and unworthiness. Standing during prayer is, on the other hand, a symbol of freedom and of the resurrection and victory. Jesus prayed both ways. He also prayed while sitting down. The Lord never legislated that this or that posture was a requisite for good prayer. Therefore, we enjoy a freedom in choosing our own comfortable posture.

However, it is always safe and sound to follow a tradition which has been blessed with years of respect and use. It is not sinful to go against such a tradition, but it is prudent to follow such a strong tradition. That is why kneeling for prayer is held in high respect.

In today's world, our bodies are given special regard and are kept trim and healthy by jogging and swimming, golf and exercise of all kinds. Therefore, the body is in good condition for kneeling, and that is an added reason (and a modern one) why kneeling is sincerely recommended. In fact, the New Order of the Mass prescribes that the faithful kneel at least during the consecration.

In brief, let the body pray by kneeling; let the hands pray by folding; let the eyes pray by lowering; and let the face pray by smiling.

7. Dedication!

There was a time when we were told that all sin was caused by the capital sin of pride. However, today when some people are not fully enlightened by the Holy Spirit, perhaps we should add to the sin of pride, another capital sin known as sloth, or just plain laziness. Are we safe to state that every sin is caused not only by pride by also by sloth? How very honest (and important) it is to admit humbly: "I am guilty of the sin of laziness." When the question of daily prayer arises, the greatest enemy those prayers encounter is the sin of laziness.

There are two phrases that are very common in today's daily language and both phrases are (after careful analysis) truly false-hoods or cover-ups for laziness. They are:

"I do the best that I can!"
"I'm too busy!"

These phrases are applied often to the recitation of daily prayers. The truth is that we seldom do the best that we can. If ever we began to do our best, we would have a new world, saturated with inner peace and tension-free vitality. In today's atmosphere, laziness sneaks in on us unnoticed. It can devour our spiritual life.

Also, if ever we began to admit that we truly are not "too busy," but that we are guilty of wasting valuable hours by means of the telephone, the TV, the coffee break, useless conversations, fooling and playing, window shopping, and so on and on, then we would be renewed by a joyful heart that would have time to accomplish the dreams of life, and the important wonders at our disposal.

Time is not accidently found; time is made. Time is made from good planning, plus honest ambition, plus sincerity, plus common sense. Just as a garden can quickly fill up with weeds, so can a twenty-four hour day quickly fill up with its special kind of weeds. Pull out the weeds and we will never need to say: "I'm too busy!"

In summary, these are the questions that have been proposed in order to clarify the modern approach to the recitation of daily vocal prayers.

1. Does God love me?
2. Have I a need to talk out to others in prayer?
3. What about discipline in praying?
4. Is there a need for variety in prayer?
5. Do I need a prayer space?
6. May I pray in bed, and must I pray on my knees?
7. Do I do the best that I can? And am I too busy?

One of the great theologians of this period of history is Rev. Karl Rahner, S.J. He wrote a book entitled *"On Prayer"* and it was published by the Paulist Press. He wrote in very simple language for very simple people about the simple aspects of daily prayer. He states (page 45):

> "We are to pray in everyday life. This should be regular prayer, practiced without regard to our humors or likings. We mean here that prayer which, without being specifically enjoined, is practiced from an innate sense of duty or as a cherished tradition—prayer at certain times, such as when retiring and before meals.

> "Prayer in everyday life includes the Angelus, the Rosary said by the individual or by the family, and visits to the Blessed Sacrament outside the times of public service.

> "Prayer in everyday life includes many pious customs we have inherited from our forefathers, such as our salutation when we pass a church or a crucifix, the sign of the cross when we cut a new loaf of bread, the blessing received at night by children from their parents. All these things are essentially prayer in everyday life. . .

> "Prayer in everyday life is difficult. It is easily forgotten, since our rushed and fevered age does not foster and promote it. It thrives only in individual hearts, which, unconcerned with the disbelief of others, can instill their own vigor into everyday prayer from their own lively and personal faith."

These words from a renowed theologian of our day lift up our hearts and encourage us to establish daily contact with God through our everyday prayers. Everyday praying is a cherished tradition and we must exercise our will to keep it an important part of our daily life.

Chapter 3

Spontaneous Prayer

Spontaneous prayer does not enjoy a long tradition among many of us. At public banquets, Catholic people used to marvel at the rather long but very beautiful and creative blessing invoked by a Protestant clergyman at the beginning of a banquet. The Catholic clergyman, at the conclusion, would often recite the usual brief and traditional prayer of thanksgiving as printed in the Baltimore catechism and as recited in a rather mechanical manner in some Catholic homes. We truly did not know whether to congratulate the priest for getting us out in a hurry, or reprimand him for being uncreative.

But that was, more or less, the way things were. Maybe long sermons were quite common, but long prayers were not common in the past among the members of the Catholic clergy. As a general rule, the priest always carried some little black book and would thumb through the book to find the correct prayer for this or that occasion. It was the Catholic Ritual, that is, the book of blessings. This is still quite common. To bless a car or to bless a home, at times the priest will still excuse himself with the simple words: "I haven't got my ritual with me. I will give the blessing some other time."

There is nothing wrong with this precise way of ministering or with one's loyalty to the ritual. Yet, surely the Lord does not limit His power only to those occasions when the blessing is read from an official book. The official book is good. We are all most grateful for the ritual. When possible, it is prudent

19

and helpful to use it. But a sincere, spontaneous prayer from the heart can surely not only touch the heart of Christ, but also touch the hearts of those standing by and listening.

The introduction of the renewal of spontaneous prayer is truly a gift of the Holy Spirit to our world of today. While it always existed, today it is more appreciated and very popular. The Holy Spirit seems to work wonders during those moments when a priest, or any individual, suddenly speaks out prayer-words from the heart which are usually so rich in meaning and so very sincere that even the one from whose heart they flow is filled with amazement. There may be stalling and pauses and grammatical errors in the spontaneous blessing, but these only add to the richness and sincerity of the blessing itself. Hesitating words coming from the heart are better than mumbled words coming from a book. A brief, sincere, spontaneous blessing, given on the occasion of the invitation, probably will be more beneficial and edifying than listening to an excuse and bringing about a postponement to perhaps a less advantageous opportunity. . .an opportunity which may never come about.

Spontaneous prayer is a form of vocal prayer. Spontaneous prayer is that prayer which is not authored formally, but which flows without effort (but sometimes with agonizing effort) or premeditation, from within a person touched by grace. Usually a sincere spontaneous prayer is prompted by the pulse of faith or the warmth of love.

Most of our common prayers come from Sacred Scripture, the Church, or the Saints. Saint Francis gave us his prayer for peace; Saint Bernard gave us the "Memorare" in honor of Our Lady; Saint Thomas Aquinas gave us many Eucharistic prayers. These and many, many other prayers the Church has officially approved and they are collected into books for our use, commonly called **prayer books.**

I personally urge each reader to ask for a new prayer book as your next birthday or Christmas gift. A good home library always possesses an up-to-date prayer book with all the traditional and recent prayers. From this prayer book, a creative person can make, up-date, substitute, and renew his or her daily list of morning and night prayers. This I stress to prove that I do not look upon spontaneous prayer to be always a substitute for our traditional prayers.

Spontaneous prayer will certainly assist in removing slipshod lip-service in our daily prayers, and will help to place a spiritual zest within them. Therefore, spontaneous prayer needs to be encouraged today among the members of the laity (and also among us priests).

By way of example, let us presume that our morning prayers are made up of the following formal prayers:

1. Morning Offering
2. Our Father
3. Hail Mary
4. Glory Be
5. Act of Faith
6. Act of Hope
7. Act of Love

As an introduction to spontaneous prayer, the suggestion is made that we pray all the memorized prayers as usual except the *Act of Love*. We can omit the formal *Act of Love* and let the heart pray out its own special prayer of love, perhaps something like this:

> "O Sacred Heart of Jesus, although I do not feel any love, I nevertheless desire to love You with my heart, my mind, and my body. You deserve my love because You have given to me a beautiful family, the security of a job, the strength that comes from good health, plus many other generous gifts. I try to follow Your example of love in loving my boss, my father-in-law, and the children next door. I especially ask for the gift of greater love. Amen."

By way of another example, let us presume that our evening prayers are made up of the following formal prayers:

1. Apostles' Creed
2. Act of Contrition
3. Memorare to Our Lady
4. Prayers to Saint Joseph
5. Prayer to the Guardian Angel

As another introduction to spontaneous prayer, the suggestion is made that we pray all the memorized prayers as usual except the *Act of Contrition.* We compose our own *Act of Contrition.* We are the ones who committed the sins; we are the ones who should pray the apology. Praying the Act of Contrition during the night prayers will be good preparation for praying spontaneously during the Sacrament of Penance. (Although the Sacrament does not require a spontaneous prayer, it is recommended.) Perhaps our prayer will spontaneously come forth something like this:

> "Jesus, I am sorry that I neglected You this day. I did not greet You this morning in prayer although You inspired me to pray when I saw my son on his knees. Now, in the quiet of this evening, I hate my sinful day: my anger at the staff meeting; my overdrinking at the party; my taking Your Name in vain while driving home with the children. I am especially sorry because You are so very generous to me and to my family. I am resolved tomorrow to pray before going off to work, and also to pray privately from time to time during the day. Without Your powerful grace, I cannot keep on the straight and narrow. Amen."

Spontaneous prayer makes prayer more personal. This personal element even influences memorized prayers and makes them more personal. It helps the lips to translate the movements of the heart. Romeo did not use memorized words of love when he poured out his heart to Juliet. Our conversations with one another are made up of spontaneous phrases which express our interior thoughts and desires and emotions. As the actor and actress must make their memorized lines sound like spontaneous phrases, so we should try to make our memorized prayers rise to God like spontaneous prayers. In prayer, let the heart and mind and lips work together like a team and offer a gift of sincere joy to God.

As we have done with the Act of Love and the Act of Contrition, so we do likewise with the other prayers. We teach ourselves the way of spontaneity in prayer. This spontaneity is not a necessity nor is it required. It is a method of vocal prayer that is recommended as a variety and to help us pray with the heart. Certainly Jesus used this form of prayer in the Garden of Gethsemani. Also, when Jesus prayed to His Father following the Last Supper (as recorded by Saint John in chapter seventeen), His form of prayer was that of spontaneous prayer.

Some may object that if each of my prayers were converted into spontaneous prayers, the time element would be stretched out too far for practical purposes. In other words, if it takes me seven minutes to pray seven morning prayers as memorized prayers, it perhaps will take fifteen minutes to pray them as spontaneous prayers. . .and I cannot afford to take that much time if I am to catch my bus at 7:10 a.m. for work.

This leads to a suggestion. Instead of giving God seven memorized prayers each morning, why not give God just seven minutes each morning. That is, pray for seven minutes each morning (either spontaneously or from memory) and stop when the seven minutes are completed, whether or not we have finished all the prayers.

In other words, I personally would prefer listening to you for seven minutes telling me a few things about yourself calmly, sincerely, and spontaneously with a heartfelt spirit, than listening to you for seven minutes telling me everything you memorized with the heart of a news reporter reading the morning news off the Q-cards.

In brief, give God so many minutes, rather than so many prayers. Give God time, not numbers. God prefers quality to quantity. Seven minutes with four sincere prayers said with the heart is better than seven minutes reciting seven prayers said with the lips (just words).

The words of Jesus in Gethsemani were few, but homilists have never exhausted their quality. His words on the cross were few, but again, homilists have never exhausted their quality. Even the words of His Mother were few, but the quality of Mary's words are ever revealing new meaning. Words of love are never rushed. God wants our hearts, not just our words.

During the era of the novena (especially in the 1930's and the depression years), the importance of numbers influenced many devout people. The novena is truly an acceptable form of prayer based on the nine days during which the apostles awaited the coming of the Holy Spirit. But in the transcendent personality of Almighty God, there are no numbers. God is not a number-God. To put it bluntly, God does not count.

Perhaps that is why God does not have clocks and calendars and calculators. Nor does God have days and weeks and years in Heaven. Quality is just beginning to seep into this planet, but quality has been in Heaven from the beginning. Therefore we need to put more and more quality into our prayers. A diamond comes one by one; coal comes by the ton. What do we prefer?

This is a listing of some helps that sum up the thoughts just presented:

1. Gradually transform some of memory into spontaneity.
2. Give God time rather than numbers.
3. Make the heart work as hard as the lips. Pray with the heart, not just words.
4. Do not let the lips do all the praying.

5. Do not rush.
6. Let prayer come from the whole self, the whole ME.
7. Do not let memory alone take center stage.

Finally, let us always remember that in our spontaneous prayer, it is the Holy Spirit ever inspiring us and moving us to say what we say, and as we say it. The Holy Spirit has no lips and no vocal cords; the Holy Spirit speaks through us.

If someone congratulates us because we prayed a very meaningful spontaneous prayer, let us say humbly only two words, no more: "Thank you!" Then silently give the compliment to the Holy Spirit abiding within us. Let us practice justice, even toward the Holy Spirit.

Sometimes it seems to me that the Holy Spirit is not an English major, and as a result, errors in proper English are made in the efforts to speak spontaneously. But an error never corrupts the message. Strange as it may seem, a slight grammatical or speaking error can (especially if it is made with the approval of the Holy Spirit) even enhance the message.

To speak spontaneously is to speak the language of the Spirit. That is the purpose for spontaneous prayer: to learn to speak His special language.

Chapter 4

Spontaneous Prayer (continued)

Because the topic of spontaneous prayer has not been treated extensively in the various manuals and books on prayer, this small primer has devoted two chapters to this form of prayer in spite of the possibility of repetition.

In the last chapter, spontaneous prayer was treated more or less from a personal point of view. The effort was made to answer these questions: How will spontaneous prayer help me in my prayer life? How will spontaneous prayer bring me closer to Christ? How can I spur myself on to use spontaneous prayer?

In this chapter, spontaneous prayer is treated from a public point of view. The effort is made to answer this question: How will spontaneous prayer help me in public or family gatherings, when a designated time is set aside for prayer?

When the chairman invites the guest to give the blessing at the annual parish banquet, the guest rises, waits for most of the people to rise, and then with the speed of a hungry laborer, blesses himself or herself and repeats traditional words which have long since lost their flavor: "BlessusoLordandthesethygifts-swhichweareabouttoreceivefromthybounty"...and this is done in spite of the fact that few can hear well, and fewer know the meaning of that strange word: "bounty."

Our Protestant brothers and friends seem to have better mastered both the art and the science of spontaneous prayer. When called upon to pray spontaneously, they rise to the occasion with the greatest of ease and pour out the most appropriate thoughts and beautiful phrases with a masterful use of the English language. I greatly admire their ability. We all have so very much that we can learn from each other.

I recall an energetic pre-med student, a Jewish convert to be, who was sharing with me his experiences about himself and his three Christian buddies living together in an apartment just off campus. "...and on every Sunday, the four of us gather in the apartment and I cook the meal of the week, a super-Sunday spread. But before we sit down, one of us is appointed to ask for the blessing...not a mechanical or artificial blessing, but a real gut-level blessing that flows out from the very insides of the fellow and has clout and sincerity, and that zips up to the Christ before we have a chance to sit down..." In other words, my friend was asking for a "spontaneous prayer" in place of the traditional prayer that has lost much of its "clout."

At one time, traditional prayer was spontaneous. Someone had to compose it. It came from someone's pen. It was printed. It was approved. It was reprinted. It became popular. It was memorized. It was handed down. It was repeated and repeated and repeated so many times that it obtained the aura of immortality.

It would not be prudent for me to define spontaneous prayer as "gut-level" prayer, so I recommend a more sophisticated definition...that looks better in print..."Prayer from the Heart."

It is my very own personal composition coming immediately and sincerely from within me, but inspired by the Holy Spirit, and addressed to the Father through Christ, both to honor Him for His love, and to ask Him for His help.

When a person stops at the parish church on the way home from work, that simple but sincere conversation directed to Christ, eucharistically present in the tabernacle, is definitely an example of spontaneous prayer. Any conversation with the Lord that flows easily and lovingly, whether it be long or brief, is spontaneous prayer.

Here is a sample of a conversation which flows easily and lovingly, not from an individual but from Christ Himself. It is a sample taken from private revelation and may be accepted or not accepted. It is a sample of Christ praying to the individual rather than the individual praying to Christ. Whether authentic or not, it is nevertheless an inspirational quotation.

> Christ speaks: "Come to Me. Show Me your poor soul. Do as the sick folk in Judea did as I passed by; talk to Me, beg Me. The gospel says, 'He healed them all.' Quicken your faith and confidence. Speak to My extravagance of love and long to respond with your own. Think of St. Francis of Assisi, the saintly missionaries and martyrs. Didn't they seem ridiculous in the eyes of the world? They were so engulfed in the love of their Savior that all things seemed as nothing to them. So don't be afraid. Take great strides toward Me. You will be richly rewarded. I could never bear to be outdone in generosity, even though I owe you nothing. Speak in your own words; make up songs and prayers for Me as they come to your mind. Be My little companion; I am yours. I have never left you since you were born, and even before you ever came into the world, I thought of you with such tenderness. Thank your God for all that came from His heart for you. Show your gratitude by asking Me to help you." (*He and I,* by Gabrielle Bossis, page 115.)

At times I hear rumblings from parishioners that they do not appreciate having a Sunday homily read word for word by the homilist. They prefer a spontaneous homily. In fact, they definitely demand a spontaneous homily, no matter how perfectly the printed homily is read, enunciated, and articulated.

Sometimes we hear our relatives rejoice and exclaim: "Oh, we had a wonderful time at the gathering. It was so spontaneous and so real."

The conclusion is that anything which is spontaneous is very acceptable.

In studying the words of Jesus, it is most obvious that when He prayed, He prayed spontaneously. Rarely did He quote the Sacred Scriptures, and when He did, usually it was within an instruction to His disciples or to the people. In His prayer to His Father, He always used His own personal composition in spite of His perfect knowledge of the Old Testament. Even when He responded to the request of His Apostles to teach them how to pray, He seemed to demonstrate His personal method of praying by spontaneously composing the words which make up the *Lord's Prayer.*

It is never a question of which is right and which is wrong: memorized prayer or spontaneous prayer, or prayer taken from a text. **All are correct.** Perhaps it could be a question of which is good and which is better. Everyday experience can give us the answer to that question. We can be thankful that our typical day is not filled with memorized statements, stereotyped phrases, and patent expressions. Even the Liturgy today gives the celebrant many, many options of expression, and encourages the one who celebrates to use the options so that variety will enhance the beauty of the Liturgy and render glory to God.

Memorized prayers are highly recommended for little children to master while their memories are blessed with their greatest capabilities. These memorized formulas will be useable in many situations as these young people grow older. For example, there are times when spontaneous prayers are just impossible, because of a headache or exhaustion, but there is a felt need for prayer. At such a time, a person calls on her or his repertoire of memorized prayers with which to contact the good Lord. Also, late at night, when one kneels at the bed for night prayers, the body sometimes just will not cooperate in conversational prayers to God and the individual needs to rely on his or her library of memorized prayers with which to express appreciation to God before retiring.

There will be a very unique time for memorized prayers, and that time will be at the hour of death or the period when death seems to be knocking at the door of one's life. What little strength there may be at the hour of death or even during the week of death is usually never sufficient for the composition of personal prayers and one must resort to memorized prayers (and many of those prayers were taught in childhood days by mother or father. What is memorized at a parent's knee will remain memorized at the hour of death.)

"But I cannot do it! I've tried! I've practiced! And I come up a blank! God will have to be satisfied with my storehouse of memorized prayers or with my prayerbook, with its many cards and copies of favorite prayers tucked inside."

That is a good, honest statement. At least this person tried. God is pleased. Probably the person will do better in the daily vocal prayers because a failure in one gift usually means a success in another gift.

There are people who just are not good conversationalists. These are quiet people, almost silent people, wishing to be interesting in conversation, but seeming almost to run out of words before they even get started. Let those people do what they do best. There is no one who can do everything. Some can do this well but cannot do that. Many cannot sing well. Many cannot preach well. Many cannot memorize well. Many cannot concentrate well. But what they can do, may they ever do it well for the glory of God. So if the honored guest at the annual parish banquet could not express with all his or her heart a spontaneous blessing for the occasion, then may the guest pray the traditional prayer with all the unction and the zeal of a veteran. God will be most pleased.

It is not recommended that an individual abandon memorized prayers or prayers read from a book, and resort only to spontaneous prayers. The two forms of praying seem to be twins: they help one another. The spontaneous prayers help the memorized prayers from becoming too mechanical, and on the other hand, the memorized prayers help the spontaneous prayers from becoming too long and too drawn out.

Very closely associated with spontaneous prayers are those prayers which you yourself compose and write down and use from time to time. Probably there are some prayers of your own composition which you even share with others. In time, the composing of prayers becomes a beautiful and useful hobby. Sometimes, a prayer can be woven into poetry and shared at Christmas, or any time. Gradually, you can compose your own little book of prayers, and meanwhile encourage others to do the same.

There are special celebrations when a definite prayer should be composed for a definite occasion, written down, and used in a fitting and proper way. Such celebrations might be:

a. Parents' silver and golden anniversaries
b. The baby's very first birthday
c. Graduation day
d. The dinner at the wedding reception
e. The banquet
f. First Holy Communion breakfast, Confirmation dinner, etc.
g. Let us not overlook the annual parish banquet next year

Returning to the question of spontaneous prayer, I wish to suggest times and occasions when such a prayer is called for and should definitely be used. These are usually occasions when, sometimes, we fail to make proper use of a golden opportunity to do spiritual good for another. Such occasions are:

a. When visiting the sick
b. When beginning a long journey
c. When sharing family anxieties
d. When storms and dangers strike suddenly
e. During a family reunion
f. Upon settling the new house
g. Around the Christmas Manger and tree
h. At the finish of a meal, social lunch, etc.

Does God want us to make use of spontaneous prayer? Is He as pleased with our simple conversations and humble compositions as He is with the inspired Psalms and many approved prayers of the Church? Yes! God has never officially made known to us His preference. He probably never will. But the history of the Church and the lives of the Saints make it very clear that He joyfully and lovingly accepts both kinds of prayers with open arms.

Saint John Climacus was the Abbot of Mount Sinai. Before his death in 649, he wisely wrote concerning prayer:

> "When you pray do not try to express yourself in fancy words, for often it is the simple, repetitious phrases of a little child that our Father in Heaven finds most irresistible.

> "Do not strive for verbosity lest your mind be distracted from devotion by a search for words.

> "One phrase on the lips of the tax collector was enough to win God's mercy; one humble request made with faith was enough to save the good thief.

> "Wordiness in prayer often subjects the mind to fantasy and dissipation; single words of their very nature tend to concentrate the mind.

> "When you find satisfaction or compunction in a certain word of your prayer, stop at that point." (Cited by Rev. Henri J. M. Nouwen, *The Way of the Heart,* page 64.)

There is no doubt that the Saints were most faithful to the "Liturgy of the Hours" and loved the recitation and the singing of the Psalms. Also, in the many writings from the Saints, it is very clear that when they prayed (apart from the Liturgical Hours) they prayed in a spontaneous way. They talked out to the Lord. The conversed with Christ in the manner of a simple, humble, human conversation. The actions of the Saints prove to us that the Lord wants this form of prayer, although His Church has not made formal pronouncements on the matter of spontaneous prayer. In this case, actions speak louder than words.

Dear Father in Heaven, thank You for giving us Jesus as Your very special messenger to planet earth. Through Jesus and His example, I have learned the meaning of spontaneous prayer. I ask for the special power to use this form of prayer in addressing Your Divine Son and His Mother, Mary. I ask that this informal, personal form of prayer may bring honor and glory to the Trinity, and may increase the friendship between Jesus and me. These blessings I humbly ask of You, Father, in the Name of Jesus, Your Son and our Savior. Amen.

Chapter 5

Recommendations

Because many individuals seldom venture beyond the tradition of vocal prayer, the following recommendations are presented so that vocal prayer can become as pleasing a form of prayer in God's ears as is possible. An ordinary glass of water given with love and refinement means more than a glass of fresh orange juice handed out carelessly and thoughtlessly.

When the Apostles asked Jesus to teach them how to pray, it is commonly interpreted that Jesus taught them a vocal prayer which, over the centuries, has been given a definite formula and which is usually recited from memory as the most commonly accepted prayer of Christianity. Jesus thereby gave prestige to this one particular vocal prayer, and today it is carefully memorized by almost every Christian the world over, and prayed daily by most Christians. By giving prestige to the *Our Father,* Jesus gave prestige to all vocal prayers. Jesus also honored the memory in permitting it to preserve the text so that it will ever be accessible to both the heart and the mind.

By giving us the *Our Father,* Jesus also set a pattern or blueprint for prayer which is often used by those who are inspired to compose prayers for general use. In summary, the prayer humbly addresses God the Father, honors Him sincerely, and then petitions for favors in a very simple and reverent manner. So in answering the request of the Apostles, Jesus gave them (and us), two answers: the perfect prayer, and the perfect pattern for prayers to be composed. Jesus also gave a unique prestige to vocal prayer.

We shall now review some of the recommendations by which we can better honor God through vocal prayer.

1. Distractions

Let us get rid of them. Let us present to God our garden of prayers devoid of the weeds of distractions. But that is easier said than done. Probably the finest remedy for distractions is the use of common sense. Let common sense be the gardner that pulls out the weeds. Common sense tells us that if we pray our official morning prayers while driving through heavy traffic, we shall be molested with distractions. Remedy? Find a better setting for the official morning prayers. Common sense tells us that if we pray immediately upon rising, while still half asleep, and without our morning cup of coffee, we shall be troubled with distractions. Remedy? Wake up. Enjoy a cup of coffee. Then pray.

Common sense tells us that if we pray evening prayers immediately after watching an exciting late movie on TV, we will be thinking more of the movie than of Him Whom we are addressing. Pause a while. Have a snack. Take a shower. Then pray. What a powerful gift common sense is. Sometimes it is referred to under the title of Prudence. Let us use it.

But if we go to our little prayer corner with the best dispositions of both body and soul, how can we get rid of those many distractions? Here are some mini-suggestions; some quick remedies:

> a. Kneel and bow your head in humility.
> b. Make a resolution: fast from day-dreaming.
> c. Fight them! ''Jesus, receive both my prayer and my battle.''
> d. Recall God's presence. (God is here. He sees. He listens.)

e. Profit from them. Accept them. Suffer from them.
f. Resolve tomorrow to prepare better for prayer.
g. Practice habitual recollection and detachment.
h. If you cannot win, then lose with nobility and with humility.
i. Jesus accepts your good intentions.
j. Distractions or no distractions...PERSEVERE IN PRAYER!

Saint Teresa of Avila has some very consoling words to share with us on this question of distractions:

> "On the vigil of Saint Lawrence, I had just communicated and my mind was so distraught and heedless that I did not know what to do. I began to envy those who lived in the deserts, supposing that, as they neither heard nor saw anything, they were free from distractions. I heard these words: 'Thou art greatly in error, daughter: the fact is, the devils tempt them more severely. Have patience; for as long as thou livest thou wilt be unable to escape from this.' While this was going on, I suddenly became recollected, and saw a great light within me..." (*Peers,* Vol. I, p. 357.)

The secret is to do the best we can to overcome distractions. But it is extremely important that we really and truly actually do the best that we can, and not use the over-worked phrase as a comfortable cushion by which to sooth a lazy conscience.

2. Discipline

The word *discipline* is related to the word *disciple.* The word *disciple* quickly reminds us of a follower of Jesus. Jesus often referred to His Apostles as disciples. We too are followers of Jesus. Therefore we too are disciples. From a human point of view, that which helps us *disciples* to follow Jesus is called *discipline.* Therefore, we need discipline if we wish to claim membership in the blessed community of those who are followers of Jesus.

Discipline is not a popular word today. For many, discipline means hard work, long hours, thankless workouts, strong language, and so forth. That which makes discipline a treasure is love.

When two people are in love, they remain in love through discipline. They are in love! He disciplines himself always to have time for her. She disciplines herself to dedicate her attention to him. Love makes discipline easy.

Spiritual discipline is also easy. It is made easy through love. If we truly love Jesus, we shall discipline ourselves never to say: "I am too busy to pray." If we discipline ourselves for love of Jesus, we shall say with enthusiasm: "Let us take a moment and pray together before enjoying our evening dinner." Discipline never permits one to say: "I forgot" or "I haven't got time."

The depth of love is expressed by the depth of discipline. The saint does not forget; the saint always has time. The saint is disciplined. The saint has a unique love for Christ. That love inspires and strengthens discipline.

Therefore, even if one's prayer life is limited to brief prayers, it requires discipline. It is that discipline, inspired by love, that brings about a strong friendship between Christ and the individual. Such a friendship cannot help but grow into a glory-filled future.

3. Children

A middle-aged man, Thomas, was at the funeral home receiving friends and relatives who were coming to express their sympathy on the occasion of his father's death. Tom's pastor had driven over sixty miles to be with him, and Tom was so grateful. He invited his pastor into a side room to talk privately about his dad.

"Father, thank you for driving all the way down here...but sit down. I must tell you about my dad. Father, on the occasion of my taking over the presidency of the Parish Council, you spoke very kindly about my faith and my love for the Church. I thank you. But now that you have seen my dad you have now seen the one responsible.

"My father was special. He was a successful business man. The bank has paid him glowing tributes. But his religion...during the twenty-three years I lived at home, I learned through him what it means to be a person of faith.

"He did all the noble things a Christian man is supposed to do. But at home, with mother and with us kids, he was a living example. Every morning and every evening, ten minutes on his knees. Never an exception. Every Christmas, even before I began school, I received a new prayer book, one suitable to my age and grades in school. Grandma used to give me ten dollars every Christmas. But dad asked her to give me 'memories' for Christmas, that is, a new rosary or a new book of one of the saints, or a medal and chain or something that would be a memory to which I could ever attach the phrase: This is a special gift from my grandparents, a special memory which I treasure.

"When I reached high school, he and I always went together on retreat. I thought that was great: rooming with my dad and praying with him and even talking about God with him. I imitated him like a monkey. He never talked in a pious way. He talked more like a man who had a close, personal friend whose name was Christ. It seems that I am catching the same spirit just by thinking of my dad.

"What he had of God he tried in every way to pass on to me. He taught by living rather than by preaching. He always listened to me more than he counseled me. Never, never once did he ever say he was too busy for me. He went to every game in which I played. While we were very close friends, he was still always my dad.

"Dad was no mystic; he was no contemplative, as far as I know. One Sunday afternoon, we were going over my childhood days, and together we counted up the many prayers he taught me over the years. I have a repertoire of exactly twenty-seven different prayers my dad taught me. . .years ago when my memory was keen and quick to absorb. Every prayer is still with me. Today, at my age, I could never conquer twenty-seven memorized prayers. But I sure am glad I have them from years gone by.

"So, Father, that's my dad. Thank you for listening to me. Memories renew me. Now that dad is gone, I hope, with God's help, to be to my children another dad like my own."

The story explains a parent's duty clearly and dramatically. For the purpose of this brief treatise, no more need be said.

4. Enthronement of the Bible

This recommendation, the Enthronement of the Bible, offers many marvelous possibilities for the family and for the home. The family and the home go together. They were among the very first creations of God. The family and the home make up the very fundamental community on which all other communities are built.

Such a community needs within the house a center or a special place reserved, as it were, for the spirit of the Trinity. The Tabernacle makes up such a center within the Church or House of God. The house also needs a center. Where can it be? What can it be?

It can be the *Holy Bible,* God's Book, the Old and the New Scriptures, always open within the house. The open Bible can symbolize the pouring out of God's Word into each floor and room and corner of the house for the blessing on the family and the home. May this particular edition of the Holy Bible be a very beautiful book, in fact the most beautiful (and perhaps the most expensive) book within the home. Maybe it is the Family

Bible given to the parents on their wedding day—one of the most meaningful gifts that can be given to a bride and groom.

But where within the house can it be placed neatly and with respect? Maybe this or that house is blessed with a prayer room. However, such a blessing is realistically reserved for few houses. Surely, after a family discussion, a corner can be found, or an area can be set aside to serve as the center or the heart of the home.

Let us for the sake of explanation select the hallway. Let us place an end table or a small decorative table in the hallway, remove from it all the accumulations of papers and pencils and other odds and ends, decorate it with a clean cloth, and honor it with the open Bible. Open to where? Maybe open it to the reading of the Nativity of Jesus or to His Resurrection. Perhaps it could be opened to the liturgical reading of the day. . .or to the readings of the Gospel of Sunday. The opening could be changed from day to day or week to week.

Why should the Bible be open? Because the Bible is God's Book. God's Book is never, never finished. It is ever a Book to be re-read. The open book symbolizes that the Word of God is to be preached all over the world, first of all, in this very house, on this very street. Like incense, God's Word will rise and go forth from this open Bible and carry its blessing everywhere. The Bible is never left on a shelf like any other book. It is not just another book. It is **the Book.** It has its own special place of honor. It brings with it God's presence, and a certain ''awe'' which makes the Christian home a kind of sanctuary. As the body is called the temple of the Holy Spirit, so too is the home with its enthroned Bible, the temple of the Holy Spirit. . .and too of the Blessed Trinity.

This special honor extended to the Holy Bible is known as the ''Enthronement of the Bible.'' It is the first step in establishing a house as a Christian Home, where the family is a community of faith and prayer. The spiritual possibilities for the family and for the home where the Holy Bible is so enthroned are many, and they are also very mysterious and powerful.

5. The Rosary

The Rosary is most certainly the "queen" of vocal prayer. After Vatican II, the queen became little by little, less popular; the world was awaiting another form of prayer to take her place. But the Holy Spirit was silent; no substitute came forth. Today the queen is regaining her beloved and well deserved popularity.

The Rosary is queen because by her fruits you shall know her. Those who pray the Rosary are strong in the faith, and loyal to their church. Some theologians and some intellectuals may have difficulties with the Rosary, but we must admit that those who pray the Rosary faithfully and devoutly are truly special individuals of faith and loyalty. They remind me of Saint Peter: they may have their short-comings, but when it comes to Christ and the church and the Holy Father, they are people of faith and loyalty.

A recent convert was experiencing great difficulty with the praying of the Rosary. In fact, she just couldn't fit it into the daily schema of prayers. But when it was learned that the vocal prayers were like a mantra or formula to be recited over and over as background music, that the thoughts or images or memories from the events of Christ's life were to occupy one's time of prayer, the convert recognized the true value of the Rosary and experienced a second conversion—to the Rosary of Our Lady.

The Rosary could almost be called a prayer of the imagination because imagination plays such an important part in creating the scenes and populating the pictures that bring to life the events of Christ's life.

If the Rosary is the queen of vocal prayer, then we are to put a royal effort into the praying of this traditional and highly respected prayer requested by Mary. Here are some suggestions:

While we commonly speak of the Rosary as a vocal prayer, it is more properly listed as a prayer of meditation. While the fingers keep count on the beads, the head paints pictures of Jesus in the various stages of His life, and the lips recite the words like a background choir of Gregorian Chant. Painting pictures is meditation, and requires time and effort and imagination. Therefore, we need to put more quality into the praying of the Rosary. That is the message: "more quality." Quality will make the Rosary one of the most beautiful queens of all prayerdom. By quality, I mean the by-product of effort and love.

A quality Rosary is known as a Golden Rosary. That is our goal: always to make every one a Golden Rosary. Our efforts will be to paint each picture, or happening, or mystery, of each event in the life of Jesus so beautifully, that we can frame it in gold as the lips softly pray the background *Ave's* of each decade. That is the Golden Rosary.

Sometimes it seems to me that it lost popularity because we lost the zeal to pray it in a quality way. It takes much effort and much love to pray the Rosary in a quality way. We cannot take it for granted. We cannot throw rags on a queen. The price of a Golden Rosary is much effort and much love. That is why the message is: more quality when praying the Rosary. As we put in, so do we take out.

6. Sunday the Sabbath

Would you be interested in restoring Sunday, all twenty-four hours of Sunday (that is, every second of Sunday, or every 86,400 seconds of Sunday) back to God the Creator, Who first created a day for Himself?

In the beginning, God the Creator gave you and me six days as our very own. God the Creator, the Father of all, then added one more day (on to the six) for Himself alone, and called that day *the Sabbath.* (We call it Saturday.)

When Jesus came to this planet, He changed the order. Jesus decided to make the very first day, His day, and to give the last six days to us. He called His day Sunday. (We call it Sunday also.) This fact is not written out in the New Testament. However, actions speak louder than words. We know Jesus chose the first day of the week as His very own, because He honored His day by rising from the dead on Sunday, and by sending the Holy Spirit to His Apostles on Sunday. The New Testament is very clear in explaining to us that the early Christians worshiped on Sunday.

It would seem that God designed the human body to be only a six-day human power. Today, we are trying to re-design it into a seven-day human power. But in time, it will be evident that the human body cannot take this extra strain, and will break down sooner or later.

Therefore, everything points to our giving Sunday back to God, and to our not stealing Sunday away from God. It is His; let Him keep it. Let us respect His possession.

While God is celebrating Sunday, how can we celebrate Sunday? Here are some suggestions:

a. Let us dedicate Sunday to rest and not to labor. We shall do what is necessary (cook the meals and wash the dishes) and avoid what is not necessary (wash the car and mow the lawn).

b. We shall make Sunday our Family Day: family breakfast; family picnic; family visits to the relatives and friends.

c. We shall dress up in honor of the Sunday Worship: traveling together to church; sitting together at church; rejoicing together at church as a family.

d. We shall slow down on Sunday and rest like God the Father: time to read the Bible; time to talk as a family; time to read a book; time to do some thinking; time to phone those away; time to meditate and contemplate; time to be a family.

e. We shall take time to do nice things: to cultivate
   friendships; to strengthen blood ties with relatives;
   to get to know one's very own family; to enjoy
   the wonders that surround all of us; to listen to
   moments of silence; to experience the love of a
   home and of a family; to listen to those special
   recordings or cassettes; and even to sit down and
   play a little music of our own, music filled with
   memories. . .

f. We shall take the time to visit the church when
   it is empty and quiet: to renew one's faith before
   the tabernacle; to pray a decade of the rosary at
   the shrine of Our Lady; to re-introduce oneself to
   the statues; to stroll along the Stations of the Cross;
   to study the architecture of the building; to be aware
   of the echos, the tabernacle light, the pipe organ,
   the windows, the characteristics that make this (my
   church), very special and different.

g. May we ever remember, that one hour in church
   for Sunday worship does not fulfill one's Sunday
   observance of the Lord's Day. There remain twenty-
   three hours and these hours also share in one's Sunday observance of the Lord's Day. It takes twenty-
   four hours to fulfill God's commandment to keep
   holy the Lord's day. It also takes planning, cooper-
   ation, obedience, and love.

Those are only suggestions. But they help to develop the men-
tality of a person of prayer. The one day dedicated to the Lord
helps to counter-act the six days dedicated to the world. It is
good to slow down: the mind, the body, the walk, the speech,
the events, everything. The faster the pace of the world, the
slower the pace of Sunday. If six days are too busy for prayer,
then make Sunday too relaxed for anything but prayer, and the
beautiful things that pertain to prayer, especially family things.

That's Sunday! That's the Lord's Day! **If our life needs prayer,
then certainly our life needs Sunday.** What a unique chal-

lenge: the honor and the joy of restoring Sunday back to God! And who will benefit the most? Ourselves!

Those are just a few recommendations by which we can better honor God through vocal prayer. It is difficult to have good music without good instruments; it is difficult to have good meals without good ingredients. It is also difficult to have good prayer without giving some attention to the various recommendations just presented. May the faithful adherence to these recommendations open up new spiritual signs and vistas for all of us which we have never known before. How God loves to come to our rescue! God is Father, and He possesses a father's concern and love for you and for me.

Chapter 6

Definition of Prayer

It is relatively easy to pray; but it is difficult to define prayer clearly and precisely. In a theological library, that section which is piled high with books is probably on the subject of prayer. An academic student, with a flair for theological research, could write a many volume series on the subject: "Definitions of Prayer in Christian Writers."

That is about what my plans call for right now: to write, not a series, but one humble chapter of a few pages on the definitions of prayer. . .and my first definition will be limited to one single word taken from the writings of Saint John Damascene who lived up to the middle of the eighth century. He wrote that prayer is simple "ASKING". . .or in Latin: *"Petitio decentium a Deo."* In the "Office of Readings," the Liturgy of the Hours quotes Saint John Damascene as practicing what he preached (or wrote) when he prayed as follows. . .a prayer reduced to the humble act of asking, and in this prayer, of asking for twelve different favors:

1. "Lord, lighten the heavy burden of my sins. . .
2. "Purify my mind and heart. . .
3. "Lead me along the straight path. . .
4. "Tell me what I should say. . .
5. "Make my own tongue ready. . .
6. "Stay with me always. . .
7. "Keep me in your sight. . .
8. "Lead me to pastures. . .

9. "Graze there with me. . .
10. "Do not let my heart lean either to the right or
    to the left. . .
11. "Let your good Spirit guide me. . .
12. "Whatever I do, let it be in accordance with your
    will. . ."

That the definition of prayer is simply "ASKING" is powerfully demonstrated in Sacred Scripture in the prayer composed by Jesus and given as a model for all prayer: *The Lord's Prayer.* In this prayer, there are seven ASKINGS. They are as follows:

1. Hallowed be Thy Name
2. Thy Kingdom come
3. Thy will be done
4. Give us our daily bread
5. Forgive us our trespasses
6. Lead us not into temptation
7. Deliver us from evil

On the night before His execution, Jesus made it very plain that His definition of prayer was also reduced to one word: "ASK-ING." The Sacred Heart of Jesus was spiritually opened wide that night with tenderness and with heroic sensitivity, and also with the deepest love of friendship as He spoke softly and calmly to His eleven in these words, repeating the very same definition over and over six times:

1. "Whatever you ASK for in my name I will do.
2. "If you ASK for anything in my name, I will do it.
3. "You may ASK what you will and you shall get it.
4. "The Father will give you anything you ASK him
   in my name.
5. "Anything you ASK for from the Father he will grant
   in my name.
6. "ASK and you will receive." (*St. John* chapters 14,
   15, 16).

While it is very true indeed that God knows every one of our needs, He nevertheless wants us to ASK. We are never to take for granted that God will automatically give us our needs simply because He possesses pre-knowledge of them through His all-knowing power. We are never to say: "I do not need to pray. I have faith that God knows what I want and will give me what I want." Rather, we are to ASK. And to ASK is to pray.

As a little boy attending Sunday School after Mass, I learned from the Baltimore Catechism that prayer: *is the lifting of the mind and the heart to God.* That too is a good definition. It is much like the simple definition of ASKING. When one ASKS, the person cannot help but lift up the mind and the heart to God. In turning to God, we admit that all good things flow from His generous hands. In lifting, we acknowledge that we have faith in God, because without faith, we would never attempt to lift our minds and hearts to the Supreme Being.

The definition properly mentions the heart. Not only do we attempt to lift up to God our understanding, memory, intellect and brain (which are included in the word, "mind"), but also our will, feelings, emotions and sensitivity (which are included in the word, "heart").

In the early centuries of Church History, prayer was primarily a matter of the mind. Early Church Fathers were greatly influenced by the learned saints who lived in the desert and also by Greek philosophy, and as a result, prayer became chiefly a matter of the mind. For the emphasis we now place on the heart during prayer, we can give much credit to Saint Bernard and to Saint Francis of Assisi and to their followers. That is why the writers of the Baltimore Catechism defined prayer as the raising both of the mind and of the heart to God.

Father Thomas H. Green, S.J. gives us two additional definitions which are a refinement on those already given here. He writes in his splendid book, *"Opening to God"* (page 31): "For some time, I have been suggesting that a better approach would be to define prayer as an OPENING of the mind and heart to God."

The word *lifting* denotes that we do the work; the word *opening* denotes that we are ready to receive from God and that we are truly responsive to God. The word *lifting* seems to mean that we are the important ones, we do the lifting, while the word *opening* seems to mean that we are in need, and that God is the important one who will fill our needs.

Father Green adds another definition for prayer and tells us that: "prayer is a personal encounter with God in love." What does that definition mean word by word?

1. *Personal*. . .that is, between God and me and us alone. God knows me, my up's and my down's, my thoughts (good and bad), my hidden deeds and my open ones, my good points and my evil points. . .He knows the true ME! And I am trying to know my true God through Scriptures, spiritual reading, prayer and friendship.

2. *Encounter*. . .that is, experience, happenings, or the effects that flow from friendship. For many good Christians, this word is relatively new when applied to prayer. The strong tradition among many is that praying is the reciting of X-number of formulas called prayers. Once they are recited, the prayer session comes to an end, and we remark: "I've said my prayers!" Now we hear that praying can be experiencing good feelings, warm emotions of love, heart-felt longings, and even the presence and the friendship of the God to Whom our prayers are addressed. Now we learn that such an experience is called an encounter. Such an experience is not necessary for good praying. However, it is not uncommon, nor should it be unwanted. As God makes use of our mind and heart, so God can make use of our emotions, our senses, our imagination and other powers of our human nature.

3. *God*. . .that is, the Supreme Being, the Almighty Father who sent His Divine Son to this planet to teach only one simple lesson, that of LOVE. This encounter takes the form of friendship because Jesus said with emotional words on that last Thursday

evening: *"You are my friends. . . I call you friends. . . You did not choose me, no, I chose you. . . (St. John:* 15, 16 sqq.)

4. *In love.* . .This meeting with God has to be in love. God knows only love. God is love. His language is love. His motivations come from love. He exists in a state of love. He who is love can only encounter in love. It is true that He came down to our level through Christ, but He now expects us to rise to His level, also through Christ.

We thank Father Green for this powerful and yet simple definition of prayer which he has given to us: Prayer is the personal encounter with God in love.

During this encounter in love, we are free to ask and to ask and to ask. Such an encounter makes a perfect setting for asking. Even in human love, asking is frequently the form taken by conversation. It was in such an encounter in love with His Apostles, that Jesus introduced the importance of asking. If prayer is an encounter in love, then prayer is the perfect preparation for Heaven where the encounter in love, initiated on earth, is continued forever and ever.

Regardless of how we define prayer, there are two elements that fit snugly into each definition and they are: "talking and listening." Prayer is a two-way street: "talking and listening." Our traditional prayer has been mostly talking. Yet, during the Sacrifice of the Mass, our traditional prayer before Vatican II had been one of listening. The perfect prayer embraces both talking and listening.

Prayer is like a two-way street: talking and listening. Prayer is also like a conversation: I talk and then listen; you listen and then talk. Prayer is not a monologue in which only one speaks. Nor is prayer a monologue in which two speak and the conversation runs along side by side. One who prays is a pray-er; one who listens is a listen-er.

How does God speak to us? He does not speak English in words which enter through the ears. He could. However, He rarely does.

God has His own unique way of communication. But because God is such a polite and courteous God, He will not speak (as a rule) unless we are listening, attentive, and willing.

"God I wish to listen. I wish to be silent. I wish only to be here in Your presence. If You talk to me or if You do not talk to me, it is still good for me to be here with You and to think of You and our friendship, and of Your goodness to me."

If it is God's will to talk or to communicate with you, it may come in various types of language-substitutes.

—He may so inspire you that you are certain it is He and not just a whim within you. Whatever manner of communication He may use, God usually makes certain that you know truly that it is He who is speaking.

—It may be so clear and strong that the listen-er dares not to risk speaking of the encounter with another, lest the other doubt or questioin the experience.

—God often speaks through a parent, or spouse, or superior, or someone who acts as a kind of messenger or angel in human flesh.

—The Sunday homily can frequently be a source of communication, unknown to the homilist and sometimes, at first unknown to the listen-er.

—God can use anything to serve His purposes of making Himself and His message known: book, newspaper, casual phone call, friendly conversation, or even something negative such as a film which unexpectedly proved not to be recommended for the general public.

—Music, poetry, literature, beauty of every kind, all can be used by God to convey a message, or to convey a mood, a consolation, or even just a wonderful feeling of goodness.

—God's YES or NO or WAIT may come to you when you least expect it, and in a way that you never imagined. He can speak in church or in a barbershop. God can give a message through the Bishop or through a mentally disturbed child. Usually, however, God is not dramatic, but is always loving. Somehow, the message is ever wrapped in love.

—It is as easy for God to come in a dream (as He often came to Saint Joseph), as it is to come through the lips of the person next door. If the message is humble, loving, simple and reassuring, then you can be certain that the message is your gift from God. Finally, if the message comes from Sacred Scripture, then you can be most certain that the message is truly your gift from God.

What is prayer? What is the definition of Prayer?
—Prayer is asking.
—Prayer is raising the mind and the heart to God.
—Prayer is opening the mind and the heart to God.
—Prayer is the personal encounter with God in love.
—Prayer is talking to God and listening to God.

If some genius could combine these definitions into one, we would then have the ideal definition of prayer. Meanwhile, we use them all. Today, use this definition: tomorrow, use that definition. Combine them; mix them; reverse them; but use them. Understanding prayer through definition will contribute a definite perspective to your daily prayers.

In brief, prayer is conversation between God and me. I pray to God and God prays to me. I talk and listen and God talks and listens. We both pray. We both converse. We both are friends and act as friends: God and I.

Chapter 7

Meditation

In writing about meditation, my sincere desire is to make this explanation very, very simple, but clear and practical. I shall limit myself to few definitions and to few divisions. A mother looks at a baby in one way; a surgeon looks at a baby in another way. I shall try to follow the example of the mother.

There are two kinds of prayer: vocal prayer and mental prayer. Up until now, we have been studying vocal prayer. It is obvious that memorized prayer and also spontaneous prayer are classified as vocal prayer. Both of them make use of the vocal cords and the lips.

However, it is taken for granted that vocal prayer has its origin either in the mind or in the heart, or in both. One who prays to God does not use the vocal cords and the lips like a parrot ...or produce the words like a cassette. The words are the expression of the mind or of the heart, or of both.

The mind does the thinking; the heart does the loving; the vocal cords and the lips do the speaking. That is **vocal** prayer.

But can one pray to God with the mind only (and just think) or with the heart only (and just love) or with both mind and heart, and never make use of the vocal cords and the lips for speaking? In other words, can a person just think or just love, or just think and love, and call that prayer? Yes, indeed! That is **mental** prayer.

To form a very simple definition, it can be stated that to think only is that form of mental prayer called **meditation.** To love only is that form of mental prayer called **contemplation.** Examples are endless...

Simple Diagram of Prayer

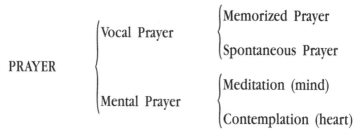

Meditating and studying are very much alike. In both cases, a person makes use of the intellect, that is, the brain, the head, the power of reasoning within. However, the purpose makes them different. They have separate goals: one goes this way and the other goes that way. The goal of studying is to acquire knowledge for the purpose of teaching, or making a living, or mastering a subject. The goal of meditating is to acquire knowledge of God and the things of God for the purpose of growing in love for God.

Meditation is not just an exercie; meditation is prayer. We often associate prayer with words formed by the vocal cords and lips. In our study of the definition of prayer, we learned that prayer is raising the mind to God or the opening of the mind to God— the personal encounter with God. Wordless prayer is truly praying, as wordless studying is truly studying.

Many truly religious people know all about this form of prayer, but perhaps never knew that it was called by the title of **meditation** in the text books and in the treatises on prayer. The story is told of Saint John Marie Vianney, the Cure of Ars, who often noticed a certain peasant praying silently in the back of the church day after day. The Cure of Ars was greatly edified by his long period of prayer and asked him what he said to Our Lord during his visit. "Oh, I don't say anything to Him," answered the peasant. "I just look at Him, and He looks at me." Apparently the peasant had progressed beyond meditation, and his lifting and opening of his mind to God had resulted in a love and close friendship that passed beyond words.

Sometimes, the secret of meditation can be lost by the use of methods which are too complicated. In the catacombs, long before libraries of books on prayer were ever written, meditation was the normal form of prayer. It was the prayer of the unlettered people. Perhaps today, certain treatises on prayer have frightened people away from meditation because the methods recommended are too mechanical, that is, too complicated with steps and divisions.

It is interesting to note that a student can spend the whole evening studying the text of the "Sermon on the Mount," for the purpose of becoming a professor of Sacred Scripture. The next morning, this student may spend the space of half an hour meditating the same text for the purpose of becoming a friend of Christ. Studying has one method; meditation has another method. The subject may be the same, but the purpose or goal is different.

What is a simple method of meditation? Let's lay out a format. However, in your reading, you may discover a method much more to your own personal liking. Follow the method that helps you the most. There is no one set method. Remember, the time may come when Our Lord will step in and guide you to a special method which He Himself will outline for you. Follow Him.

1. It is more or less taken for granted that you have chosen a quiet place for meditation: your room, the church, the park or lakeside, the family room in the early morning, in your car parked beside a vacant lot, and so forth. . .True friendship and true love always finds a place where this friendship and love can grow and mature. Such a place not only benefits one's meditation,

but also benefits one's nervous system and mental health. Ours is a big world, and there is a "desert place" somewhere.

2. It is most helpful to impose the spirit of discipline and to establish a definite period of time to be given to the meditation: fifteen minutes each day, half hour on Saturday and Sunday, or ten minutes every morning before work, etc. In living a truly spiritual life, we must never belittle the importance of discipline. In setting a definite time schedule, it is my own personal opinion that the period of meditation should seldom be less than fifteen minutes daily. The daily time schedule that seems most common and traditional is the thirty minute period each day.

If an individual has reached the age of retirement and if God has graciously bestowed the gift of extra hours each day upon that person, then, in love and in justice, it seems that thirty minutes given to meditation could easily be a discipline that is imposed with joy and appreciation. Years of retirement should be looked upon as joy-filled years of spiritual growth and loving maturity as one prepares for the glories of eternity in Heaven. On the night before His execution, Jesus said to His Apostles and also to you and to me: *"All this I tell you that my joy may be yours and your joy may be complete. . . that joy no one shall take from you."* (*John* 15:11, 16:22).

3. Saint Teresa writes: "It is a great help to have a good book, written in the vernacular, simply as an aid to recollection." (*Way of Perfection, Peers,* Vol. II, page 109.)

Personally, I recommend from the very start, that the "good book" to possess is the book of books, the Holy Bible. And from the Bible, I recommend (for the beginner, at least) the New Testament. And from the New Testament, I recommend the four Gospels. Let Matthew, Mark, Luke or John be your companion in your daily meditation.

Probably the most popular edition of the New Testament is the New American Bible. It is this edition that is most commonly used in the daily Liturgy. While every edition could probably be recommended, it is wisely suggested that the New American

Bible be used in order to harmonize the Bible language of your New Testament with the Bible language of the daily Liturgy.

To be very honest, almost any spiritual book could become a "good book" to act as an aid to meditation. This is the opportunity for sharing. Maybe the book that helps one will help another. Never in the history of Christianity has there been so many excellent pieces of literature on spirituality, as there are in these final years of the twentieth century.

This need for a good book leads to the building up of a small but very selective spiritual library. I am not recommending that you join a book-of-the-month club right now. Now is the time to be sharing and to be selective. All this takes money. Books are expensive. But the investment is not only a necessity, it is a tremendous means of companionship, security, and peace.

I go so far as to recommend a budget just for spiritual books. Begin with the classics written on the spiritual life. Buy them. They become like brothers and sisters to you. They become books you share but you do not sell or give away. Establish your own book-of-the-month club and sign up as your one and only member, and obtain a book each month. Or establish your own book-of-the-every-other-month club if your finances are low, and be faithful to your commitment.

The secret is: have a good book to aid you in meditating. If your meditation becomes filled with distractions that just will not go away, then you read. Reading dispels distractions. Reading controls the mind and the imagination and forces them back to the task of meditating. The book is the officer in charge of distractions, and is to be summoned each time the distractions get out of control. However, one must be watchful that the reading does not substitute itself for the meditation.

4. Our Faith teaches us that God is Trinity: one God and three Divine Persons. It is very helpful for meditation to direct our time for meditation to One of the three Divine Persons: to the transcendent God the Father to Whom the prayers at Mass are

ever directed; to Our Lord and Savior, Jesus Christ, Who visited our planet to teach us love and to be our forgiveness; to the Holy Spirit Who dwells among us to guide us along the paths of love; or to the Holy and Blessed Trinity.

If we chose to open our meditation with a spontaneous prayer to the Blessed Trinity, perhaps we could pray spontaneously something like this:

> "Heavenly Father, please hear my prayer. During these moments of meditation, send forth the Holy Spirit to assist me. I ask this sincerely through Jesus my Savior. Amen."

In brief, we are free to open our meditation with prayer to 1) the Trinity, 2) the Father, 3) Jesus Christ, or 4) the Holy Spirit. We may also direct our prayer to Our Lady or to one of the Saints. They in turn will intercede in our behalf.

Certainly, a traditional prayer or a memorized formula may be used in place of the spontaneous prayer. However, as one grows from vocal prayer to mental prayer, it is advisable that one also grow gradually into spontaneous prayer. Such a prayer inspires a person to be fresh and new and creative. It spurs us to rise out of a routine which can plunge a person into an unproductive root.

5. The opening prayer leads us into the reality of the Holy Presence of God. Saint Paul told the philosophers of Athens, *"God is not really far from any one of us. In Him we live and move and have our being."* (*Acts* 18:27-28). The foundation is the doctrine of God's omnipresence, that is, God is everywhere. Being very human, we easily and quickly forget His Presence. But we cannot escape Him. We may forget Him, but God cannot forget us. He is beside us, above us, in us, beneath us, around us, and with us. He is everywhere and we are in His midst. To recall this fact is to practice the exercise of the Holy Presence of God.

Our opening prayer helps to emphasize the exercise of the Presence of God because we are told in *Psalm* 145:18-19 that *"The Lord is near to all who call upon Him. . . He hears their cry."* We also recall that the Three Divine Persons abide within us by God's gift of grace. We may not understand this because it is a mystery. But this we believe because Jesus said on the night before His execution, concerning a person who will love Him: *"We shall come to him and make our home with him."*

I highly recommend the book titled: *"The Practice of the Presence of God"* by Brother Lawrence. It is one of the great spiritual classics. It would be an excellent book to have in one's spiritual library to be read and reread over again.

6. On what text or subject shall we meditate? To what page shall we open our book? To what chapter shall we open our Bible? Those are questions that should be settled before beginning the meditation. The following are some directions on where to discover, or on how to determine the subject for meditation.

    a. Take one of the assigned readings from the daily Liturgy for your daily meditation.

    b. Take one of the four Evangelists and meditate through the Gospel, covering as many verses as possible, slowly and reverently and meaningfully.

    c. Interrupt your schedule from time to time with a special meditation on subjects like these:
       —The Saint of the day, or the season of the year
       —Special event, local or otherwise
       —An inspirational hymn, or a special program of the Bishop
       —A worthy news event, a war, a death, a tragedy
       —A birthday, anniversary, or holiday

    d. Use any section of the Bible that is an inspiration to you.

    e. Perhaps in some cases, the subjects will be selected by one's spiritual director. In that situation, be obedient; do as you are directed.

Again, I repeat that the subject should be selected before one settles down to meditate. Meditation time should never be used to "hunt up" material for this particular meditation. Time set apart for meditation is already too brief to be used for making a selection, or for picking out a theme.

In a small notebook or in one's journal, it would be helpful to record neatly and carefully, a list of your personally selected topics for meditation. A review is always in order.

I shall close this chapter by reviewing the six steps in preparing for meditation. These steps may appear to be complicated in the beginning, but in time will flow forth quickly and easily. . .so quickly and easily that it will almost remind one of the simplicity of preparing the early morning snack known as breakfast. The steps are:

1. Choose a quiet place for meditation.
2. Through discipline, establish a definite period of time.
3. Have a good book, including the Holy Bible.
4. Dedicate, through prayer, the time of meditation.
5. Practice the Presence of God.
6. Select the subject for meditation before beginning the period of meditation.

Chapter 8

Meditation (An Example)

To make the preparatory steps for meditation more realistic, it is helpful to imagine someone actually talking with us about his experiences in attempting to meditate. With the assistance of our imagination, we picture a rather young husband and father addressing us in words something like these. He speaks to us:

Everything is ready for my daily meditation. The six steps have been completed. I am sitting in the family room downstairs where all is quiet, especially at 7:00 o'clock in the morning (Because my neighbor picks me up for work at 8:15 o'clock).

These few minutes of meditation are dedicated to Christ because I feel comfortable with Christ, knowing that He abides in me. My prayer is spontaneous and it goes something like this:

> Jesus, I dedicate these few minutes of meditation to You. May they honor You in some small way! May they also help me to know You better in order to love You better! This request I ask of Your Father and my Father in Your Name. Amen.

The text is the continuation of the Gospel according to Saint Luke. For some weeks now I have been covering about one paragraph of this Gospel each day. By using this method, the text is always ready. However, usually I read over the text as a part of my evening devotions. If I am alone, I read it outloud. My wife is also attempting to meditate each day, and while we do not meditate at the same time, we do try to follow the same text each day and to proclaim the same text together each night. I seem to receive more insights when one proclaims and the other listens. It seems to be the meaningful way to bring the day to a close and to give a blessing to a new day to come.

The text we read last night and the text I am using this morning is as follows:

> The reading is from the Gospel according to Saint Luke, chapter 4, verses 42, 43 and 44.
>
> 42 *The next morning Jesus left the town and set out into the open country. The crowds went in search of him, and when they found him they tried to keep him from leaving them. But he said to them,*
>
> 43 *"To other towns I must announce the good news of the reign of God, because that is why I was sent."*
>
> 44 *And he continued to preach in the synagogues of Judea.*

There are a few observations which may be of value to you. I wish to state with great joy in my heart that my wife and I have been deriving great benefits from our daily meditation. The benefits cannot be measured but they can be observed. We have learned to share. She shares with me, and I share with her. We have learned to share spiritual matters. She is not my spiritual director, but she comes close to this ministry. We feel comfortable in talking about the things of God and about our inner feelings and emotions. We are closer. And the children are grasping the idea of sharing by just living in an atmosphere of sharing...especially my oldest son who is only sixteen. It's great! I never would believe it if I did not experience it!

In conclusion, there is a strange difficulty which I should perhaps mention. It is a difficulty which both my wife and I have been experiencing. The strange difficulty is this. Meditation (as we understand it) does not seem to be quite enough...I mean to say...meditation (as a means of knowing Christ) does not quite satisfy. . .as if there were something else we are missing. But what is this something that we feel is lacking? What is it? That is our difficulty. What is this something?

What is this something? The answer is very simple. It would seem that both the husband and the wife are ready to pass from the prayer of meditation to the prayer of contemplation. The prayer of the mind is quickly preparing them for the prayer of the heart. They are growing. In the spiritual life, they are growing in a very simple and normal way. There is nothing extraordinary in their spiritual growth. The head is giving way to the heart. Thinking is giving way to loving. Meditation is giving way to contemplation.

Let us go back briefly and review the definition of meditation, the true meaning of meditation. (Contemplation will be explained in the following chapter.) We have learned that meditation is truly prayer. . .prayer without words. It is a form of mental prayer that makes use of the intellect, the brain, the head, the power of reasoning within. This is a quotation of what we have read: "The goal of meditation is to acquire knowledge of God and the things of God for the purpose of growing in love for God and in friendship with God. . .Meditation, therefore, is reflective prayer." Meditation gives us knowledge of God, and the more we come to know God, the more we shall eventually come to love God. That is the secret: . . .come to love God. So, our goal eventually is **love**.

In brief, we are here in that level of spiritual growth where we are seeking knowledge of God; we want to know God, so that latter, we shall use that knowledge to love God. In many situations, as we know God, so do we love God. So let us hurry to know Him and to know Him better.

How does the passage taken from Saint Luke (chapter 4, verses 42-44) help us to know God?

That passage taken from Saint Luke is inspired. That means that God, by His infinite supernatural power, in some mysterious way, moved Saint Luke to write verses 42, 43 and 44. Saint Luke wrote (in his own unique style of writing) exactly what God wanted him to express. One could say that the content, thoughts, and lessons were touched by the all-powerful hand of God, and delivered to earth through inspiration. Saint Luke was the human instrument that rendered that inspired message readable to us of this world. Maybe Saint Luke misspelled words. Maybe his grammar was not good. Maybe Saint Luke, as God's chosen instrument, had poor sentence structure. Nevertheless, he delivered God's message as God wanted the message to be received. In brief, the message of those three verses are inspired. Through meditation, we attempt to comprehend the message, and to appreciate God and the things of God more and more. Then, later, with what we know, we shall begin to love. And God is Love!

Realizing the meaning of inspiration gives the book a holiness and a prestige which sets it aside from all other books. It is THE BOOK! That is why the Bible is honored within the home by having it enthroned in a place of distinction. That is why it is not enough just to read the Bible; the Bible should be meditated.

During the Sunday Liturgy, we notice the honor given to the reading of the Holy Gospel of the Bible. Only the celebrant reads the Gospel from the Bible. The celebrant bows in prayer that he may be worthy to proclaim the Word of God. He greets the people and calls them to attention with his exclamation: "The Lord be with you!" He leads the people in making the triple Sign of the Cross on the forehead (that we may understand the Word of God), and on the lips (that we may speak well the Word of God), and over the heart (that we may love the Word of God). Out of reverence, we stand and listen. Sometimes, the Holy Bible is honored with incense and with candles. After the proclamation, we are seated while the celebrant explains the Gospel just read. Such an explanation is known as the homily. This is the way the Church honors the inspired message. And by the enthronement of the Bible, our homes honor the inspired message, that is, the Word.

So we look upon these three simple verses with awe! They are inspired. Their content is from Heaven. They are filled with the infinite power of God. They have a message. Through meditation, we unravel that message, and learn about God and about the things of God.

On occasion, we hear some very good persons say that they truly "get nothing out of the Bible." The Bible is something like classical music: the more we try, the more we appreciate. On May 15, 1897, her last year on earth, Saint Therese of Lisieux shared with her sister:

> "As for me, with the exception of the Gospels, I no longer find anything in books. The Gospels are enough. I listen with delight to these words of Jesus which tell me all I must do: *'Learn of me for I am meek and humble of heart.'* Then I am at peace according to His sweet promise: *'And you will find rest for your souls.'* "

When Saint Therese quoted the last sentence (her eyes raised with a heavenly expression in them) she added the words 'little' to our Lord's words. "And you will find rest for your little souls." (*Her Last Conversations*, translated by Rev. John Clarke, O.C.D., page 44)

A story is circulating around about a dear old lady who died and was welcomed by Jesus with open arms. Jesus knew that there had to be judgment, but His desire was to make it short and also sweet. So He asked a very simple question of the dear old lady: "And did you read My Book?" and the answer came back: "Dear Jesus, I never knew You wrote one!" I do not know whether or not her answer was a sufficient excuse, but I do know that it is wise to have read at least the New Testament before having our heavenly interview with the good and kind Lord.

We shall not take the time here to meditate in depth those words quoted according to Saint Luke. Here we shall only attempt to draw forth some of their rich meanings, a few of their hidden

meanings. Every simple word is inspired. Every single word holds
more than meets the eye. Meditation (with the light of the Holy
Spirit) draws from each word those many meanings and paints
a picture far more fulfilling than the simple message seen by
the eyes alone. In brief, let us now ask the mind, the imagination, the memory, the whole head to search out each word that
is seen by the eyes. In other words, let us meditate. . . Let us
know Christ in a more meaningful way in order to love Him
in a more personal way.

Enrich your meditation by asking these questions concerning
the three verses quoted previously according to Saint Luke.

1. Where did Jesus spend the night? In a house?
   Under stars? With Peter?
2. Jesus must have left the town all alone by Himself. What time was it?
3. Jesus must have left very early before the crowds
   got up.
4. Did He have breakfast?
5. What is meant by the "open country?" Was this
   a place of prayer?
6. The country could not have been very open if
   people went in search of Him.
7. Did Jesus want to get away to be alone with His
   Father? Why?
8. Did Peter also go in search of Jesus?
9. Did Peter's mother-in-law go in search of Jesus?
10. How many went in search of Jesus? Five or ten?
    Maybe two hundred?
11. Would I have gone had I been there?
12. Where did they find Jesus? On a hill? In a valley?
    In a cave?
13. When they found Jesus, was He walking, resting,
    praying, eating, running?
14. Was Luke perhaps one of the people who went
    in search of Jesus?

15. How did they try to keep Jesus from leaving? What did Peter say?
16. If you were there would you have done most of the talking?
17. Do you believe that Jesus should have remained with them? Why?
18. Was Jesus impatient with them? What was His attitude?
19. What towns do you think He was talking about?
20. What is the "good news" about which Jesus is speaking?
21. What is meant by the "reign of God?"
22. Is the "reign" the same as the "kingdom" mentioned in the Lord's Prayer?
23. Who sent Jesus? Why was He sent?
24. What are synagogues? Where is Judea?
25. God is Love! How is Jesus showing and providing the meaning of LOVE?

Fifteen minutes are hardly sufficient time to cover even three verses. The above questions and statements read more like a class in exegesis rather than a meditation to bring about knowledge of Christ. However, the questions and statements help to open up the Scriptures. Once the Scriptures are opened up, then we sit back and begin to **know** Jesus.

Look into the word "know" and the word "knowledge." It has been stated clearly that the goal of meditation is to know God and the things of God, or, in other words, to have knowledge of God. I am not speaking of speculative knowledge or theoretical knowledge. I am not trying to use meditation as a means of making a walking text book out of the one who meditates. The knowing of which I am writing is to experience Jesus, that is, to acknowledge Him and to accept Him because of this knowledge. To "know" (in the Biblical sense) is often a gift, that is, a charism acquired from the Lord and not acquired from investigation. This knowledge is the fruit of faith, experience, and God's generosity.

Saint Paul writes to the Corinthians that his knowledge is imperfect now. However, he adds that in Heaven he will know God as God knows him. His words are: *"My knowledge is imperfect now; then I shall know even as I am known."* (*1 Cor.* 13:12). This is the kind of knowing that is meant to be the fruit of meditation. We seek to know Jesus in order to love Jesus, not in order to teach about Jesus. We seek that knowledge which eventually makes its way into the heart, and not knowledge which remains stagnant within the intellect. The goal of meditation is knowledge that goes forth like an apostle, not a knowledge that stays at home like a scholar. We need the scholar and we need the apostle. Meditation, however, prefers the apostle.

"Where did the time go?" Meditation seems to swallow fifteen minutes or even thirty minutes in one quick gulp. Once a person adopts meditation as a way of prayer, it is almost impossible to say: "Oh, I forgot!" or "I just haven't got time!" All good things, however, have an ending. How does one bring about this ending? When time strikes fifteen or thirty, the ending is brought about with two simple steps:

1. The offering of a simple **resolution** based on the meditation.
2. The offering of a short but heartfelt **prayer**.

A resolution is a souvenir that is carried with you in your memory at least during the day. The secret is to keep it simple. Another secret is to keep it realistic. You are the one who is to keep the resolution.

Many individuals keep a spiritual notebook, commonly known as a journal, in which they write down inspirations, resolutions, and spiritual happenings. I cannot encourage too highly the use of the journal every day, or at least every week. The journal should be some kind of a notebook of good value, worthy of the contents. Many bookstores now carry the journal in many designs and with happy colors. One who meditates can be certain that there will be high spiritual events in her or his life, and it is profitable to date them and to write them in the journal, even in shorthand or in a foreign language if so desired. A last thought on the journal is this: the journal makes a splendid and appreciated gift.

The meditation is then closed with a very simple prayer. Often, a person over-meditates and is forced to close the period hurriedly. Therefore, a short prayer is usually the best prayer. A short prayer that is prayed well is far better than a long prayer that is prayed poorly. Again I shall give a list of suggestions or examples:

1. The Lord's Prayer
2. The Memorare
3. The Glory be to the Father
4. The Prayer of Saint Francis
5. A spontaneous prayer to the Trinity
6. A spontaneous prayer to Our Lady or a Saint
7. The Sign of the Cross

Let us keep in mind that, after all is said and done, the very best resolution and the very best prayer is that which circles around the gift of love. The Act of Love is highly recommended as a closing prayer.

Brief Outline of the Prayer of Meditation

I. PREPARATION:
1. Chose a quiet place
2. Establish a definite period of time
3. Have the Bible or a good book
4. Dedication
5. Practice the Presence of God
6. Have the subject for meditation selected before beginning
II. THE MEDITATION
III. CONCLUSION:
1. Resolution
2. Prayer

Chapter 9

Contemplation

Please do not permit the word **contemplation** to frighten you. Contemplation is a form of prayer which is not beyond you, nor too much for you, or a form of prayer meant only for Trappists and Contemplative Nuns and other monastic religious. Both the word "meditation" and the word "contemplation" have turned many noble people away from God's generous invitation, but probably the word contemplation has been the greater offender. Maybe it is the evil spirit that places a certain fear in these words.

Also, perhaps some spiritual writers down through the ages have sincerely defined contemplation in such sublime terms that generous people have been frightened away. "Contemplation is not for me!"

In brief, while meditation is the prayer of the intellect, contemplation is the prayer of the heart. After all is said and done, and after pages and pages of explanation have been written, the simple truth is that contemplation is simply the prayer of the heart. . .or the prayer of love.

If you experience satisfaction with that simple definition, you need read no further. However, I feel a calling to write out a more detailed explanation for those who wish to delve deeper into the rewarding gift of contemplation. May the good God give me the gift of simplicity, so that what is written may be written in a clear, straight forward, and practical way.

70

Endless definitions have been given to contemplation. In spiritual writing there is a kind of confusion as to what precisely contemplation truly is. Perhaps it could be said that contemplation is that prayer which follows meditation. After a period of time spent in meditation, there is a hunger for something else. What is that something else? The person who shared with us his experience in meditation admitted that he and his wife experienced a need for something else. After weeks of meditation, they experienced a lack of something. What was that something? Because knowing leads to loving, that something which they both needed and lacked was the prayer of love, the prayer of the heart, which is called contemplation. It is the prayer which follows meditation.

While it is said that contemplation follows meditation as loving follows knowing, nevertheless, the two work together like twins. One needs the other. The more one knows the more one can love, and more one loves the more one thrives to know. But in the end, love takes over. Love is the stronger of the two. The love that is born on earth lives on forever in Heaven. In Heaven there is no faith; there in only love. We do not need faith when we possess the object of our love, and that object is God. And God is LOVE.

God, in His infinite goodness, does not permit a definition to keep generous individuals from entering into contemplation. I recall a very generous woman of little formal education who made her way daily to Mass and to the Eucharist. As she received Holy Communion, the tears of love were always creeping down her cheeks and the love she experienced was clearly written in the expression in her face. She approached the reception of the Eucharist in a state of contemplation, but if she were asked about how she felt, surely she would be confused and wonder why anyone would pick her out as special or different. Her experience she could never define, nor would she want to define the way she felt. Probably, she would answer in all her simplicity: "I just love Jesus!" She was most certainly a contemplative

and didn't know it. And she didn't need to know it. Jesus was
leading her.

Father Henri J. M. Nouwen writes clearly and beautifully about
this "prayer of the heart" and I wish to quote generously from
his book, *"The Way of the Heart"* (Ballantine Books, pages 59
and 60.)

"For us who are so mind-oriented, it is of special importance
to learn to pray with and from the heart. The Desert Fathers
can show us the way. . . .We find the best formulation of the prayer
of the heart in the words of the Russian mystic Theophan the
Recluse: 'To pray is to descend with the mind into the heart,
and there to stand before the face of the Lord, ever-present,
all-seeing, within you.' . . .Prayer is standing in the presence
of God with the mind in the heart. . .

"We have to realize that here the word heart is used in its full
biblical meaning.

"In our milieu the word heart has become a soft word. It refers
to the seat of the sentimental life. Expressions such as 'heart-
broken' and 'heartfelt' show that we often think of the heart
as the warm place where the emotions are located, in contrast
to the cool intellect where our thoughts find their home.

"But the word heart in the Jewish-Christian tradition refers to
the source of all physical, emotional, intellectual, volitional and
moral energies.

"From the heart arise unknowable impulses as well as conscious
feelings, moods and wishes. The heart, too, has its reasons and
is the center of perception and understanding. Finally, the heart
is the seat of the will: it makes plans and comes to good deci-
sions. Thus the heart is the central and unifying organ of our
personal life. Our heart determines our personality, and is therefore not only the place where God dwells but also the place
to which Satan directs his fiercest attacks. It is this heart that
is the place of prayer."

In brief, the heart is I! The heart is ME! The heart is where my office is found. If you want to discover the true ME, look in my heart. When Jesus comes to me, He comes to my heart. He abides in my heart. When I say that I love Jesus with all my heart, I mean that I love Jesus with all the powers and strengths and faculties and gifts that have their headquarters within my heart. I love Jesus with all of ME.

Let us in a brief, simple way, experience a contemplation.

In preparation, we can follow the same opening steps we used for meditation. For our text, let us select the nativity passage as found in the Gospel according to Saint Luke, chapter 2:

"Mary gave birth to her first-born son and wrapped him in swaddling clothes and laid him in a manger."

Because this is a contemplation, let us be inspired by the words of Saint Ignatius in his Spiritual Exercises, where he speaks of the "contemplation to attain the love of God." That is, briefly speaking, the goal of every contemplation: to attain the love of God.

Saint Ignatius also encourages a person to use the imagination in trying to attain this love of God. Although the word imagination is not used in this contemplation of Saint Ignatius, he takes the imagination for granted. For example, in contemplating the Christmas scene, he explains that the point of this contemplation is to look at the Holy Family (imagination), and three of them, Jesus, Mary and Joseph. Saint Ignatius further explains that I am to pretend that I am just a little person (imagination) standing reverently before the Holy Family, looking at them, contemplating them and even serving them (imagination) with as much reverence and respect as possible. To carry out these recommendations of Saint Ignatius demands great use of the imagination, all of which will lead a person to attain the love of God. So the contemplation begins:

I tiptoe up to the manger. (I make every action as of the present. I am in the manger here and now. I am not looking back into

history. I am present in the making of history.) A light shows
me the way. But where does the light come from? It is so quiet.
I see Mary. She is holding the Child. Joseph is standing beside
her watching and protecting as it were. Mary looks tired. The
Baby is asleep. Can I talk? Should I talk? What should I say?
How do I greet this holiest of families? But I don't have to speak.
Mary smiles and then speaks so softly I can hardly hear: "Come!
Welcome! Our very first visitor!" Joseph comes to lead me in.
I cannot talk. I just look. And wonder! And feel what I never
felt before: the experience of love! Nothing happens. We all
remain like statues. But I do not want anything to happen. I
want this experience of love just to continue on and on and
on. . .Why must anything happen? Yet, Mary looks so tired. I
cannot believe that it is I who break the silence. I speak. I cannot believe that I am speaking. I ask: "Mary, may I hold the
Baby? You are tired. Do take a rest."

Now Joseph is speaking. What a mellow voice he has! He speaks
with a smile. I am attracted to this man as never before. I never
knew Joseph very well. He inspires me. He is speaking: "Mary,
the two of us will prepare a place for you. Then you can rest."

I spring up quickly as if out of a dream and follow Joseph to
the back of the cave where we both come to life and work with
a zeal and a love that never before spurred me on. And we hurry:
cleaning away the cobwebs, inviting the bats to leave for a while,
removing the dung, leading the animals further back, gathering
some straw, pulling some grass, making a resting place for the
new mother, and then washing my hands and my arms in the
nearby stream so they would be somewhat worthy of holding. . .of even touching the little One, Mary's Baby, my Lord
and my God. . .

Mary only says two words: "Thank you!" as she places into
my arms, my very arms, the sleeping Child. Joseph smiles a warm
smile of approval. Mary turns back to me and whispers: "Sometimes the Baby falls back to sleep better hearing a melody with
a few simple words of love. . ." And Mary leaves me with the
Baby. I am all alone with the Child. He is so loveable. He is

so loving. He is God. I am without a prayer. I cannot talk. I am holding Love. I experience...that is all...I experience...and now He opens His eyes. They are so small, so powerful. They look through me. Is this the time to sing? But He keeps looking. Why do I wish He would look somewhere else? His look is so strong! And He is only a Baby. Maybe His look is His way of asking for a song. He asks for a song and I ask for a voice with which to sing a song. And all of a sudden out flows...

Silent night...Holy night...All is calm...All is bright...And the Baby seems to smile. Is he smiling in love or smiling at my off-key singing? But He closes His eyes...He seems to have fallen asleep...But His love seems to continue to fill me with an experience that only Heaven experiences without end...

Two hours have passed...and Mary returns...and I fold the Baby into her arms...and...

My contemplation of fifteen minutes is over...so quickly...

And so I conclude:

1. Lord, only one resolution can I make from this contemplation and that is the resolution to love...

   a. On leaving for work, I shall look into the eyes of my wife; I shall smile at her; and I shall kiss her with love.
   b. On arriving at work, I shall give the doorman not only a "Good Morning!" but also a pause in place of a rush.
   c. Each person on the staff will receive a "Good Morning" with the spirit of love, and each person will also receive a pause to frame the greeting with sincerity.
   d. The morning coffee break I shall spend alone in contemplative prayer; the afternoon coffee break I shall spend with the staff in the spirit of Christian love.

e. Each of my children this evening will receive from me the gift of personal time and personal interest in the form of personal love from me to each.

2. Lord, my concluding prayer will be directed to Your Mother. I shall pray her *Memorare* with all the sincerity that went forth from the heart of Saint Bernard who composed the prayer, and who passed it on to us.

It is very possible that the person who made such a contemplation is filled with anxieties and worries over many, many situations. The person needs God's gracious help. The burdens of life are piling up and his dreams are falling apart. Such a person may prefer to close the contemplation with a spontaneous prayer like this:

> Jesus, I love You and I know that You love me. You have called me: Friend! I call You Friend and more: I call You my Lord and my God. With humility, I ask for Your powerful help. I ask You to touch with Your healing hand my mother and heal her or, if it be Your will, take her joyfully to Heaven. Jesus, I ask You to abide within our staff at the office and give us harmony, good will, and success. Jesus, inspire my wife and me to live out our vows of our marriage in a Christian way and so renew the dreams of our marrige day. Lord, keep drugs and alcohol, and premarital sex away from our home. Take our children into Your arms and hold them in safety. Amen.

Compare meditation and contemplation and study how they differ and how they are alike.

They differ in many ways of which these are but a few:

1. In meditation we think and we study as it were. In contemplation we use the imagination and permit the imagination sometimes to drift off into a kind of spiritual daydream.

2. In meditation we look into the past as a rule. Not always is there a sharp, clear-cut difference between meditation and contemplation. They can overlap at times. In contemplation we look into the present. As in the contemplation just presented, I am holding the Baby in my arms right now in this present moment.

3. In meditation we look in at the scene. We study the picture. We look up the situation. In contemplation, we get right into the scene. We are actually in the picture. We are a part of the picture before us.

4. In meditation we seek to know. We want knowledge. We want to know Jesus better. We long to have a greater knowledge of Jesus. In contemplation we want love. We want to love Jesus better. We long to have a greater love for Jesus.

5. Meditation is discursive prayer. We go from point to point. In our grasp for knowledge, we go step by step and page by page as we make progress through reasoning. Meditation covers broad areas. Contemplation is affective prayer. It is prayer of the heart. Emotions and feelings play an important part in affective prayer. The area may be smaller, but the depth may be deeper.

6. Meditation makes great use of the intellect. Contemplation makes great use of the will.

7. Meditation is the tool of the theologian and of the student. Contemplation is the tool of the saint.

These points can be summarized in this way:

MEDITATION:	CONTEMPLATION:
Thinking	Imagining
Studying	Spiritual day dreaming
The past	The present
Looking at the scene	Entering into the scene
Knowing	Loving
Discursive	Affective
Intellect	Will
Tool of the theologian	Tool of the saint

In evaluating the two forms of prayer, is one greater or more valuable than the other? Yes. Contemplation is the greater. Why? Because the object which is love is greater than the object of meditation which is knowledge. Love prompted God to create us in the first place. Love moved the Father to send His Son to us in order to restore us. Love moved Jesus to save us and to give Himself to us as our Spiritual Food. Love moves the Holy Spirit to abide within us and with us and to guide us in all ways. Heaven is love. God is love. Love is the only thing that gives meaning to life. Contemplation is one of the most valuable spiritual tools that leads us to greater love.

It was Saint Theresa of Lisieux whom God sent to teach us of the twentieth century, the secret of love. She died just three years before this great century opened, but she left us her story in book form, and she wrote to us as follows:

> "As I meditated on the mystical Body of Holy Church, I could not recognize myself among any of its members described by Saint Paul...Charity gave me the key of my vocation. I understood that since the Church is a body composed of different members, she could not lack the most necessary and most nobly endowed of all the bodily organs. I understood, therefore, that the Church has a heart—and a heart on fire with love...Beside myself with joy, I cried out:

> "O Jesus, my Love, my vocation is found at last—MY VOCATION IS LOVE! I have found my place in the bosom of the Church, and this place, O my God, You Yourself have given to me: in the heart of the Church, my Mother, I WILL BE LOVE...Thus shall I be all things and my dream will be fulfilled." (Chapter XIII, *A Canticle of Love,* page 203, from the autobiography published by P. J. Kennedy and Sons, New York.)

The 1930s will be remembered as the decade of the novena. The novena is truly an acceptable form of prayer and petition. However, over the years, the novena influenced our way of thinking in regard to our petitioning God for assistance in our many needs. Never explicitly, but surely implicitly, many individuals began to feel that God is moved by numbers. The more we say and the more we repeat, the more God is moved to come to our rescue. We forget that the language of God is love. The secret is: the more we love the more God comes to our rescue. In the hectic rush of our world, it is difficult to recall that God is love and Heaven is love and that God hears best, as it were, in an atmosphere of love. Contemplation is meant to bring about that atmosphere of love. Petitions presented to God within this atmosphere of love (whether through novenas or contemplation) cannot but be heard by God. However, there is no guarantee that any and every prayer reaches God. But, we can be humanly certain that all prayers wrapped in love reach the loving heart of God. Such prayers are both heard and answered.

We were introduced to contemplation through the nativity passage found in the Gospel according to Saint Luke. With the help of our imagination, we entered the cave and held in our arms the Christmas Infant, Our Lord and Savior, Jesus Christ. We even attempted to sing to our eternal God the only song we knew, and we experienced the meaning of love. Our goal was reached, and our goal was love. And we resolved to live a life of love at the office and at home.

We shall now briefly look at other passages from Sacred Scripture which can be contemplated and which can lead us to love, both to experience God's love and to encounter that love.

1. In the Gospel according to Saint Luke we read: *"Jesus went down with them then, and came to Nazareth, and was obedient to them. His mother meanwhile kept all these things in memory."* (2:15 and 52). For your contemplation, visit Mary at her home. Sit down and share with her all these things she kept in memory. What were the very first words Jesus spoke? When did Jesus take His first steps? How did Jesus as a little child help His mother? Abide with Mary and grow in love for Jesus as His Mother shares many things from her memory.

2. In the Gospel according to Saint Matthew we read: *"Then Jesus was led into the desert by the Spirit to be tempted by the devil."* (4:1). For your contemplation, do not seek to know more details about the adventure, but spend at least one day and one night with Jesus in the desert. How does He respond to your words of sympathy? What does He say when you give Him a little basket of fruit, or when you ask to help Him, or when you suggest that you remain with Him? Where do you stay for the night? What is the desert like? Is the hungry Jesus as loving as the Jesus resting at the home of Mary, Martha and Lazarus? Do you leave Jesus with the experience of greater love?

3. In the same Gospel we read: *"Seeing the crowds, Jesus went up the hill. There he sat down and was joined by his disciples. Then he began to speak. This is what he taught them... (Matt.* 5:1-2). Sit as His feet. Look into His eyes. Bring Him a cup of fresh water. How does He show appreciation? Are the crowds listening? Does Jesus say anything of a personal nature just to you? Do you encounter spirit of great love in the words of Jesus? Does He look upon the crowds with love? Do you feel the warmth of His love within you? Do you say anything to Him? Do you ask for any special favor?

4. In the Gospel according to Saint Mark we read: *"Seeing the Apostles tossed about as they tried to row with the wind against them, Jesus came walking toward them on the water...When they saw Jesus walking on the lake, they thought it was a ghost...They had all seen him and were terrified."* (6:48-50). How come you are in the boat? Are you frightened with the storm? Are you rowing? Is that figure over there a ghost? Are you terrified? Are you going to scream? Jesus is pointing to you. He is asking you to walk on the water with Him. Are you going to walk with Him? Is the lake now calm enough for walking? If you go walking with Jesus on the lake, what are you going to talk about? Will you be too frightened to talk? Why is Jesus walking on the water with you and not with Peter or John? Under such circumstances, does Jesus still radiate love? While

out in the lake, do you still experience His powerful love? Are you growing in love for Him as He walks with you on the lake?

5. In the Gospel according to Saint John we read: *"Jesus rose from the meal and took off his cloak. He picked up a towel and tied it around himself. Then he poured water into a basin and began to wash his disciples' feet and dry them with the towel he had around him."* (13:3-5). Jesus is calling you. He is calling you from the kitchen into the banquet room to have your feet washed with the Apostles. What do you say to Jesus? Are you surprised at the invitation? Do the Apostles say anything to you? Do you notice Peter or John? Do you notice Judas? Does Jesus say anything special to you? Are you moved by His concern and His love? Are you more and more attracted to Jesus? Do you wish that you were an Apostle? Does this happening increase your love for Jesus. Why?

6. In the same Gospel we read: *"I give you a new commandment: Love one another. Such as my love has been for you, so must your love be for each other."* (13:34). As you stand in the kitchen, can you hear Jesus say this? Do you see anything new in this commandment? Does it go into one ear and out the other? Are you permitted to come into the banquet room and sit down and enjoy the rest of the discourse of Jesus? Are you getting much out of His words? Do you think His words on love are the high point of His conference with His Apostles? Do those words of Jesus at the Last Supper help you to love Jesus with any greater love?

7. In the Gospel according to Saint Luke we read: *"When they came to Skull Place, as it was called, they crucified him there. . .Jesus said, 'Father, forgive them; they do not know what they are doing."* (23:33-34). For your contemplation, go to Calvary on the First Good Friday. Can you hear Jesus saying these words? Are you standing near the cross? Is John there, and Mary His Mother? Can you speak to them? What do you say to them? Do they share with you? Do you shed any tears? Are you frightened like the other Apostles? What are your thoughts? Do you think Jesus sees you standing there? Does Jesus say anything to

you? Do you believe that Jesus has a personal love just for you? Do you have a truly personal love for Jesus? Have you any resolutions to prove your love for Him? Do you honestly believe that you and He are true friends? Is Jesus dying?

With the help of these examples, it becomes very clear that contemplation leads to love. This method of prayer makes a powerful use of one of God's greatest gifts to us, our imagination. With our imagination we burst right into the scene. We are not interested in the past or the future. We walk into the present scene and take a definite part in the scene. We are looking for love. We want to encounter love. We desire to experience love. . .and a particular kind of love, namely, *the love of Jesus.* Almost every passage in Sacred Scripture can lead us through contemplation into the heavenly spirit of true love.

Does the prayer of contemplation fit into our definition of prayer?

Prayer involves asking! Once we encounter Jesus in love through contemplation, we experience the freedom of asking and asking and asking. Where there is love there is freedom to ask. Those who love are made happy by asking, and by being asked.

Prayer is raising the mind and the heart to God. In contemplation we raise the mind, but especially the heart, to God. Contemplation and meditation often walk together just as the heart and mind walk together. They are like twins and twins help one another. But there are occasions when one twin is invited to do a little more than the other. In contemplation, it is the heart who does the larger portion of the work.

Prayer is opening the mind and the heart to God. And never is the heart permitted to open wider than in the call to contemplation.

Prayer is the personal encounter with God in love. Such a definition could well serve as the definition of contemplation. If we do not encounter God in contemplation, then perhaps we have failed in some way or manner. Perhaps that is a sign that we should evaluate our manner of prayer and seek the guidance of the Holy Spirit. Surely a conference with a spiritual director would be in order.

In conclusion, let us ever remember that everyone is called to contemplation. Contemplation is never reserved for a choice few. It is open as the generous arms of Christ. He calls everyone. He invites everyone. He wants everyone because He loves everyone.

Chapter 10

Other Forms of Contemplation

How truly grateful I am to God for permitting me to live during these closing years of the twentieth century. When I was first ordained to the priesthood, stationed at the parish of my assignment was a petite Trinitarian Sister by the name of Sister Thomas Augustine. She was so little that one had to check one's sneezes and coughs lest she be blown away and lost. But what influence she exercized over the little ones and the poor of the parish! It was she who taught me to have a strong, living devotion to the Holy Spirit. But in those days, the Holy Spirit was the unknown Person of the Trinity. How I longed for the day when the Holy Spirit would dominate the whole Christian world and be known and honored and loved by every Christian. Then, back in the 1960's, the beloved Pope John XXIII opened the windows and in flew the Holy Spirit.

It is the Holy Spirit Who has inspired many changes in this era, especially within the Church. In a letter to his priests dated January 15, 1986, Bishop Matthew H. Clark of Rochester, writes on the question of change and explains that change is not a "fearsome and threatening event" but rather "an experience of walking with the Lord to new life."

It was the Holy Spirit Who invited the people of the Lord to walk with Him to new life when He inspired the great Ecumenical Council, the twentieth in the long history of Christianity. Now we are privileged to live in, and to benefit by, these rich post-conciliar years. Of all the blessings the Holy Spirit has sent upon us, the greatest seems to be that of new insights and new interests and new depths in our lives of prayer. Today we can enjoy the experience of walking with the Lord to a new life of prayer.

Never in history have there been so many books written on prayer, so much interest in prayer, and so very much growth in prayer. In the past there were great giants of prayer and the Church has honored these giants by declaring them saints and doctors. But today, the growing interest in prayer is shared with the religious, the clergy, and above all, with the men and the women and also the children who sit in the pews, and who serve the Church in so many noble ways.

As a young boy in the grades, I knew many prayers from memory as I have explained. But I no longer crowd my prayer period with memorized prayers. Now I am reaching God through many other meaningful ways of praying, ways that are certainly not new but perhaps not popular, and which have experienced a resurrection during this glorious era of prayer. Some of these ways or forms of prayer are:

— Spontaneous Prayer
— Meditation
— Contemplation
— Faith sharing
— Centering Prayer
— Prayer of Quiet
— Prayer of the Heart
— The Jesus Prayer
— Prayer Groups
— Contemplation Groups
— Prayer with oriental techniques
— Lectio Divina of the Benedictine tradition

Now we can better appreciate the power of *opening a window!*

Let me make it very clear that I still use memorized prayers that my mother taught me years ago. I shall never, never abandon them. Nevertheless, how happy it makes me to realize that there are other ways, many other ways, to pray to God. And it is my desire to share with you, not all, but some of these other ways.

Perhaps it would be more accurate for me to stress that it is my desire only to introduce *some* of these other ways to you. To write fully about all forms and ways and methods of prayer would require books. This is only a simple primer. But I wish you to be aware of the existence of various methods of prayer. For the present, I shall write only a simple introduction to a few ways of prayer with the hope that over the years, you yourselves will become better acquainted with each of these ways or forms of contemplative prayer.

Each of these types of prayer could be listed under the general heading of contemplation. As we recall, contemplation is that prayer which follows meditation. Once we get to know God honestly and truly in meditation, then we long for more, and that more is to experience the love of God in contemplation. True knowledge leads to love, as meditation leads to contemplation. Knowing leads to loving; meditation leads to contemplation.

Contemplation reminds me of candy. As candy is of sugar, so contemplation is of love. Just as there are many kinds and forms of candy, so are there many kinds and forms of contemplation. Let's look at some of these forms of contemplation.

1. Centering Prayer

Centering Prayer is not new. The method of Centering Prayer is defined in great detail in one of the outstanding spiritual treatises of fourteenth-century England, "The Cloud of Unknowing," whose authorship remains unresolved.

The purpose of this form of prayer is to obtain love. Ever remember that one request made with love is worth more than any other request made with hours of lip service.

On that night before His execution, Jesus spoke out His heart to His Apostles. Meditate deeply on these words of Jesus (repititious though they may seem) and try to unravel their meaning:

> *Make your home in me as I make mine in you.*
> *Remain in me.*
> *Whoever remains in me, with me in him, bears fruit.*
> *Who does not remain in me. . .withers.*
> *Remain in me.*
> *If my words remain in you. . .*
> *Remain in my love.*
> *You are my friends.*
> *I call you friends.*
> *I am in my Father and you in me and I in you.*
> *If anyone loves me. . .we shall come to him.*
> *If anyone loves me. . .we shall make our home with him.*

Where is this remaining going to take place? Where will the Three Persons center Their activities and remain in me? Where can I find the Trinity within me and where can I center my attention and center my love for Jesus? Where is the place or the center of our remaining, of our loving, of our friendship? And the simple answer is: the heart. . .my heart.

So I go to my heart, that is, to the center where all of me converges. There I find Jesus; there I find the Trinity; there I find love.

But too often, it seems that our heart is covered somehow with a cloud, that make it difficult to penetrate and to find love. That cloud seems to be of a strange, unknown kind that forces one to speak of it as the "cloud of unknowing."

But my love for the Trinity is so demanding that I am willing to make every effort to penetrate that cloud of unknowing to find love. I find the Trinity being at home or making home within my heart. I find love taking over and I encounter the gift of peace, the kind of peace that only the Trinity can give because this peace flows from our love. I reach my goal on earth, and I long for my permanent goal of love in Heaven.

That is Centering Prayer!

But oh! the distractions that keep me from piercing the cloud of unknowing with my feeble love. How wild my imagination becomes! My memory begins to bring back the past with its evils and its sins and its dangers, and I seem to lose my way as I try to pierce the cloud and find love.

If I am bothered with all kinds of distracting thoughts, the author of the book has some practical suggestions. (This suggestion is found in chapter 7.)

> "When you set yourself in this exercise. . . lift up your heart to God by a humble impulse of love. . . A simple 'reaching out' directly towards God is sufficient. . . If you like, you can have this reaching out wrapped up and enfolded in a single word. So as to have a better grasp of it, take just a little word, of one syllable. . . Such a one is the word 'God' or the word 'love'. . .This word is to be your shield and your spear. . .With this word you are to beat upon this cloud. . .With this word you are to strike down every kind of thought. . ."

The simple little word is repeated softly and slowly over and over in order to drive away the many distractions. The word is so simple that it forces us to be humble. The word is so powerless that it forces us to let go. . .We who are so very ambitious and who have everything under our control are truly forced to let go and to let God take over. So we continue to repeat the word like a little child. We add a bit of love now and then and from time to time a bit of trust. In time, we penetrate the cloud of unknowing and there we find love centered in the heart. Our love meets the transcendent love of the Trinity and rests without a word. And all is centered in my own little heart. . . in me. . . in the total me!

According to the Trappist monk, M. Basil Pennington, O.C.S.O. in his excellent article, Centering Prayer—Prayer of Quiet, ("Finding Grace at the Center," page 9), this beautiful form of prayer derives its title from Father Thomas Merton. Father Pennington writes:

> "This simple method of entering into contemplative prayer has been aptly called **centering prayer**. The name is inspired by Thomas Merton. In his writings he stressed that the only way to come into contact with the living God is to go to one's center, and from there pass into God. This is the way the author of 'The Cloud' would lead us, although his imagery is somewhat different."

This is Centering Prayer and it is for everybody. It is not a special gift of God to a few, but to the many. However, it is very true that there may be those who are not attracted to this particular form of prayer. This should never disturb anyone because God, in His generosity, has lavished us with several methods and forms of prayer, of reaching Him, of sharing with Him. We are free to choose that type of prayer which harmonizes best with our personality and our natural characteristics. While Centering Prayer is one of the very best ways in which to meet with the Lord, it does not stand alone. It is one of many. God calls His people to Himself in various, wonderful ways.

2. Prayer of the Heart

For me, to be an instrument of the generous Lord to introduce to others the various rich forms of prayer is truly a tremendous joy and satisfaction. Too many zealous Christians have only known vocal prayer; too many have been frightened away from contemplative prayer. This new Pentecost, which is truly a golden era following the Vatican Council, has opened up these many forms of contemplative prayer to the people of the pews. These people, who work hard during the week and who struggle daily with modern living, are now encouraged to practice the prayer forms of the centuries. My dream is to do my small part to make these methods of the past better known to the present.

In the early days of Christianity, prayer was regarded primarily as an activity of the mind or the intellect. Prayer was the conversation of the intellect with God. However, in the fourth and fifth centuries, religious writers looked upon prayer as an activity of the heart.

By heart is meant more than the emotions and the feelings. By heart is meant the whole human person: the body, the soul, the all of a person. This is the interpretation of heart in its full Biblical meaning. When I say: "I love God with all my heart!" I mean that I love God with my intellect, my soul, my body, my senses, my feelings, my emotions, my strengths, my weaknesses, my all. The heart is the center of the whole person, everything leads to the heart. A person who prays with the heart is a person who is totally identified with this form of praying, **Prayer of the Heart.** it is very self evident that this form of prayer is almost the reflection of Centering Prayer.

The heart is not only the center of the human person, it is also the dwelling-place or the abiding-place of the Trinity. The heart becomes the place where the created (myself), meets the Uncreated (God). Both God and I meet in the heart. Our meeting place is in the heart. The heart is the office in which God and I transact our spiritual business—and other business as well.

Our conversation is in the heart, a soundless, silent conversation, and that is the meaning of Prayer of the Heart. We appear before the Triune God abiding within the heart. We are one! (Cor ad cor loquitur! Heart speaks to heart!). The way to God is through the heart. Saint Paul writes (*2 Cor.* 13:5): *Perhaps you do not realize that Christ Jesus is in you.*

God is not just another problem that our mind has to deal with. God is with us and in us and behind us and before us. This inspires us to hide nothing from Him and to surrender ourselves totally to Him. How encouraging are the words of Jesus: *Blessed are the pure of heart: they shall see God.*

In his excellent little book, "The Way of the Heart," Rev. Henri J. M. Nouwen develops these thoughts and teaches us how to practice the **Prayer of the Heart**. The book is highly recommended.

As with all types of prayer, discipline is demanded. God's generous grace works best with discipline. Nothing great comes easy in this world. All great things demand discipline, even the Prayer of the Heart. Every disciple grows through discipline!

Here are a few simple suggestions for those who may wish to begin now to attempt to pray the Prayer of the Heart:

1. Keep everything simple. Be utterly alone with God.
2. Speak but little: "My God, I believe!"
3. Very little: "Mercy!"
4. Love is speechless. Love is silent.
5. Love is non-active. Accomplish only love.
6. Ask for this. Just a word.
7. Ask for that. Only a word.
8. Repeat TRUST to dispel distractions.
9. Rush nothing, relax.
10. This is true contemplation.
11. This is the prayer God wants.
12. This is how Mary prayed.
13. This is heavenly love. This is heaven on earth!

Then take all thirteen of these suggestions and try to incorporate them into every aspect of your daily life, because prayer of the heart is the process of making God the first priority in everything you do, every day of your life.

3. The Jesus Prayer

The Jesus Prayer takes us to the people of the Christian East, especially to the Orthodox tradition where Jesus is invoked primarily through frequent repetition of the Jesus Prayer. The standard form consists of ten words:

"Lord Jesus Christ, Son of God, have mercy on me!"

The origins of the Jesus Prayer are traced to the Desert Fathers of the fourth century. But in all honesty, it goes way back, as far as the Bible itself. The prayer was used in the monastery of Saint Catherine, on Mount Sinai, and in the fourteenth century, on Mount Athos, in Macedonia, which for centuries remained the center for the offering of the Jesus Prayer. This little prayer was received with great enthusiasm by the Russian Orthodox Church and was given widespread recognition and use. The Roman Catholic and Protestant traditions did not bring the prayer to western Christendom until the middle of the twentieth century. So the journey of two thousand years saw this little prayer travel from the Holy Land to Mount Sinai to Mount Athos to Russia and finally, to the English-speaking world of the West.

The prayer opens with the lips. The lips say the words that form the prayer. The prayer is said again and again and over and over and over. Sometimes a prayer-rope is used, or a rosary. Repetition is the rhythm of the prayer. But eventually, the prayer must be prayed from the heart through the lips. The prayer soon begins to take on the nature of **Prayer of the Heart.** How does all this come about?

As we well know, what exactly is meant by 'the heart' is not easily defined. Just as the heart is the organ of life, so the heart is the center of personality. We love with all our heart. We strive not to be a heartless person. We want greatly to be an individual who has heart, and has a heart in the right place. We do not desire to be heartless under any circumstances.

So we take this little prayer and we go into our heart as one goes into his or her room and there we shut out all distractions and meaningless memories and pray within the privacy of the heart: "Lord Jesus Christ, Son of God, have mercy on me!" And we say it again and again and again, and we remain so busy saying the prayer that distractions and memories have no chance to invade the privacy of our God, and of us in private prayer. Jesus tells us: *Whenever you pray, go to your room, close your door, and pray to your Father in private. Then your Father, who sees what no man sees, will repay you. (Matt.* 6:6).

In other words, whenever we pray the Jesus Prayer, we go to the room of our heart, close the door of our heart, and pray to the Father from within the heart. Then our Father, who sees within the heart what no person sees, will repay us.

Gradually, the prayer becomes more a prayer of the heart than a prayer of the lips. It blocks out the distractions; it keeps out the memories. It closes the lips to conversations. It turns off the intellect to discursive reasoning. It quiets the nervous system and relaxes the body. And alone with God in the closed sanctuary of the heart, the prayer is offered: "Lord Jesus Christ, Son of God, have mercy on me!"

With its roots in Scripture, with its acceptance primarily in monastic life, and its growth chiefly among the Eastern Orthodox people, is this form of prayer meant for me? The question reminds me of a graduate student at one of our universities, inquiring about his praying, as he walked from lecture to lecture across the rather extensive campus. I recommended the Rosary of Our Lady and the Jesus Prayer. The Jesus Prayer was new to him. But after trying it he became greatly attracted to the prayer and remarked. "I have become struck by the amount contained in so few words." And soon the Rosary was being prayed as he walked across the campus in one direction, and the Jesus Prayer was repeated as he returned across the campus in the opposite direction.

But is this form of prayer meant for me? Yes! Definitely! Try it! It grows on you! Here are a few quick and easy suggestions to assist in praying the Jesus Prayer:

— No preparations are necessary. Just . . . pray.
— Pray without ceasing. It is a one breath prayer.
— Pray while you work. Pray while you drive.
— Pray while you golf. Pray while you converse.
— Use in meetings, lectures, workshops.
— Pray while you wait.
— Pray while falling asleep.
— Pray on waking up.

— Use in jogging, practicing, playing.
— Pray in waiting rooms and airports.
— Pray in doctor's and dentists' offices.
— Pray during hurried times. Pray when sick.
— Pray when tempted. Make every breath a prayer.

Presently, there are a number of books and pamphlets on the Jesus Prayer. All of them seem to be very well written. The traditional book, first printed back in 1884, is written by an unknown author. The manuscript came into the hands of a monk at Mount Athos. The English title was "The Way of a Pilgrim," and was translated from the Russian. It offers an excellent and practical introduction, in story form, to the Jesus Prayer.

4. "Lectio Divina" (Bible Reading)

In the early centuries of Benedictine monasticism, the monk's daily service of God was threefold: 1) prayer, 2) manual labor, and 3) reading (lectio divina). In those same early days, reading was considered the most typical monastic element in the life of a monk. Today, some monastic prophets speak of this reading as a thing of the past.

What made this reading (commonly called even today: lectio divina) so very important? We can appreciate its importance better if we realize that lectio divina was limited to the reading of Sacred Scripture. This reading was not about one's apostolate or about the martyrs of former times or about the history of various movements; this reading was Biblical. Furthermore, the reading was not for scholarly or academic purposes; it was for one's own spiritual growth. Usually, the only other readings apart from the Bible were those of the Fathers on the proper interpretation of the Bible. Some of the Fathers described their conversion, either to Christianity or to the life of a monk, to their having turned away from secular literature to the reading of the Scriptures. This encouraged many monks who, in the beginning, had a kind of repugnance for the Bible. Saint Benedict so greatly appreciated the importance of this reading that his rule allots some four hours daily to reading, and much of the time was set aside in the early morning hours, which were more condusive to Biblical reading. Today, many read the Scriptures just to know what they can do with the words they find there. Such was not the case with the monks in early monasticism. They were truly concerned with what the Scriptures were able to do with them and for them.

In our present vocabulary, "lectio divina" is commonly translated as "spiritual reading." However, it is evident that this is not a good translation, nor is it a correct translation. Lectio divina was defined in the early days as a kind of slow meditative reading of the Scriptures to obtain a personal contact with God. Spiritual reading today is much broader, and embraces a much wider horizon.

In lectio divina, the monk was not just reading documents of the past; the monk, as it were, got into the very documents themselves, and discovered themselves in Daniel and in Stephen, and in the early community life of the Christians. They found Biblical texts to justify every monastic activity even if it meant, at times, going a bit to extremes. In brief, the monks put themselves on the stage of biblical history and lived as if the history of salvation was continuing in them.

Probably the closest we come today to lectio divina is the practice of meditation. If we could spiritualize our study of Scripture a little more and study it, always in order to better live it, perhaps biblical studies could then approach the early meaning of lectio divina.

What can we learn from our own sanctification from a study of the lectio divina of the early Benedictine rule? Here are a few recommendations.

   a. We can be inspired to look upon the bibilical texts as the very best source of material for our meditations and our contemplations. Learn to love the Bible.
   b. Spiritual reading as defined today is still important. We definitely should read the lives of the saints,

especially the saints of our own era. Saints are given to us not only for the sake of intercession, but especially for the sake of imitation. Build up a library of spiritual books.

c. We can appreciate the importance of discipline in the spiritual rhythm of our day. Resolutions need to give way to discipline. Fasting is the teacher of discipline.

d. There are two descendents of lectio divina: studies and spiritual reading. Maybe we could learn to fuse them together or bring them closer so that our theology could become more spiritual and our spiritual reading could become more theological. In short, theology should not just be another course for which I gain so many credits toward my degree. And spiritual reading should not be just another book report.

e. As a child in my home (a good Catholic Irish home), we never had a Bible. The Bible was so special, that the thought never came to us that we, ordinary people, could have a bible within our house. The Bible was an awe, a reverence, a respect, a holiness that made it too much beyond the possibility of ever having one of our own. My first Bible came to me when I was in college. I am not recommending a return to that situation. I am, however, recommending a return to a greater respect for the word of God. It was a Protestant woman who inspired me to respect the Bible after I had carelessly stacked some secular books on top of the Bible. She corrected me, kindly and lovingly. I was well into my priesthood before I learned to encourage the enthronement of the Bible in every home. In brief: reverence!

I visited the Benedictine monastery of Mount Saviour to inquire about lectio divina. The prior, Father Martin Boler, O.S.B. immediately said to me, ". . .and the modern translation of lectio divina is Read God!" I have been meditating that phrase ever since.

How beautiful! How meaningful! Read the message of God as He speaks to us in the trees, the horizon, the faces of brothers and sisters, the birds flying south and the sheep in the pasture, the headlines of the daily papers, the sick, the old, the little ones, the people we meet and the letters we receive. God is ever speaking, never silent. He surrounds us with His message. Read God! Read His message! Read His writing! Read His Word! What a perfectly glorious, powerful, awesome translation! Read God! So that is the modern translation of lectio divina. Read God Who has written and recorded a message in everything, and sometimes even in nothingness. No wonder Saint John writes: *"But these have been recorded to help you believe that Jesus is the Messiah, the Son of God, so that through this faith you may have life in his name."* (20:31).

5. Faith Sharing

Under the title of Faith Sharing, we can gather together many beautiful forms or kinds of prayer which belong, more or less, to the same family: 1) Shared Prayer, 2) Shared Contemplation, 3) Praying the Scriptures, 4) Benedictine Method, 5) Prayer Groups, 6) Contemplative Groups, and others.

During the three months while Mary was staying with Elizabeth, the two of them must have shared their faith and their prayers. Surely they invited Zechariah to sit in with them, and he, good man that he was, must have shared his faith and his prayer with them by means of a writing tablet. In Nazareth, I cannot imagine Jesus and Mary and Joseph sitting alone, night after night, in absolute silence without sharing with one another. Today, we imitate their good example in our faith sharing groups.

Not everyone experiences the call to this form of prayer. There are private people, who, by nature find sharing very difficult. During His three years of public ministry, Jesus seldom shared His prayer with His Apostles. It was more common for Him to go by Himself, away, and there to spend the night in prayer to His Father. But for those who like to gather to pray together, here are a few helps. There is no definite way. Your way is as good as this way. Do as the Holy Spirit speaks.

    a. Select a leader who will notify the group as to the place, time, duration and special needs for a particular session.
    b. Each participant should have a copy of a uniform Bible, for example, the New American Bible.
    c. The gathering place should be warm, quiet, comfortable, and acoustically fit with good hearing facilities.
    d. The leader asks:
      —That everyone be comfortable and relaxed.
      —That everyone observe the sounds of silence.

This particular form of prayer has been attributed to Saint Benedict. It is obvious that it is related to his "lectio divina." It usually is divided into three parts:

    1. "Lectio" (lectio divina or spiritual reading or Scriptural reading)
    2. "Meditatio" (that is meditation)
    3. "Oratio" (the prayer)

The passage from the Bible has been selected by the leader who has already appointed someone to read. The reading is done three times, either by the same reader, or by three appointed readers. It is always better to appoint than to ask for volunteers— the asking can often be very disturbing. The three proclamations by the lectors have a stronger influence on a listener than three silent readings by the individuals. Also, each reading is interpreted in a different way. The leader will have instructed the participants in these various ways.

    a. 'Lectio':
      1) The first reading of the chosen text pertains to the WRITER. Why did the writer record this one particular passage? What is the message to be presented? What would the writer have to say about this particular chosen text? Etc.

2) The second reading of the same text pertains to the HEARER—to ME. What do I get out of this passage? What does the message mean to me? What do I think of this text? How does it move me? What is my felt reaction? What happens inside me? Etc.

3) The third reading of the chosen text pertains to GOD. Why did God inspire this passage and have it recorded for posterity? How is God moving me as it is read the third time? What do I experience God saying to me? Am I able to listen to this reading as a letter written by God to me and to me alone? What does God want me to notice? Etc.

b. "Meditatio and/or Contemplation": (Period of sharing)

Then follows a period of complete silence, the length of which is determined by the experiences of the individuals and by the good judgment of the leader. The time is dedicated to:

1) Meditation, that is, thinking and using the intellect and mind on the Scripture passage just read, not for the purpose of passing an examination, but for the purpose of knowing the Lord and knowing what He wants of me. Why did God inspire the writer to record this passage for me? What does that tell me about the Lord?

2) Contemplation, that is, I may discontinue my meditation, and, with all my heart, enter into contemplation so that, knowing the Lord better, I can now love Him better. I rest in love. The silence of the gathering moves me to love. The message of the passage had brought me to love. From meditation, I pass quickly into contemplation.

During this silent period, sharing is always acceptable. Sharing is not indicated by the raising of the hand or by the nodding of the leader. Sharing is the spontaneous unction of the Holy Spirit. If the meditation moves you, speak out and share what moves you. If the contemplation moves you, speak out and share what moves you. This encourages others. This is not a distraction. Your comrades came to share, to encourage one another, to help to lift one another's mind and heart to God. So share: briefly, lovingly, softly and sincerely. When others share, listen attentively and make what they share your very own. Let the community be one. Let his sharing and her sharing be your very own sharing, and then rejoice that God is in your midst, and that sincere minds and hearts are being lifted high to Him. If you experience the inspiration to remain silent, then remain silent. (However, silence is the exception.) In your silence, smile and rejoice that you are in the midst of hearts where God abides and makes His home, and where love is the bond of union.

c. "Oratio" (Prayer sharing)

As the designated time begins to draw to a close, talk to God in prayerful words: briefly, spontaneously, and with the unction of love. Ask for your special favors. Mention by name those in need. Speak out your prayer for the benefit of others, if you are so moved. Let them, by their "Amen," join in your prayer and be a part of it...as you can be a part of theirs. The prayers of the participants should bring about the most meaningful inspirations of the session and help to unite the participants into a loving body of praying Christians.

The session closes with utter simplicity: the participants rise, reach out for his or her neighbors' hands and with hands joined and heads bowed, pray the "Lord's Prayer," concluding with a slow, reverent Sign of the Cross.

Jesus said:

> *Where two or three are gathered in my name, there*
> *I am in the midst of them!*

Isn't there a lot of similarity in these various forms for prayer? Yes! Absolutely! That is why this chapter includes them under the umbrella of contemplation.

These forms are, in a certain sense, different views of the same; different reflections of the same; or different ways of observing the same. Each has some of the ingredients of the others. All are pathways leading to the knowledge and love of God. Each is trying to bring a little bit of Heaven down to earth. Each tries to give us a peek into the windows of Heaven and to experience a touch of the glories of Heaven. To contemplate does not mean that we follow this method on every Monday, and that method on every Tuesday, and on and on. . .With this knowledge of many possibilities, let the Holy Spirit lead us to that form of prayer, or to that combination of forms of prayer, that accommodates us. I am me, and you are you, and you are to pray as YOU. The Holy Spirit, Who knows you well, will accommodate you with a way of prayer which can give you a taste of Heaven right here on earth. TRUST THE SPITI!

Chapter 11

Spiritual Direction

For me, Our Lady has always been the model of prayer, both meditative and contemplative. Our Lady has also given me (and all of us), the secret of spiritual direction. This secret is hidden in her last recorded words lovingly preserved by the one who made his home with her, Saint John. The words are:

"Do whatever he tells you." (2:5)

With these words, Mary appoints her Son, Jesus, the Spiritual Director of each of us. This may sound pietistical, but it is practical, realistic, and after all is said and done, the only solution to the question of spiritual direction.

When I was in the seminary back in the 1930s, a priest was always appointed by the Bishop to be available as the spiritual director for the students. There was no obligation to chose him as one's own personal spiritual director, but, on the other hand, he was a good priest, convenient, accessible, usually in his office, and always willing to sit down and hear one's confession or talk things over. Most of the students chose him, either officially or unofficially, and at least visited him weekly for confession.

After ordination, people approached me and asked me if I would be their spiritual director. In practice, that meant would I be in the confessional box each Saturday for confessions. If so, the individual would make plans to come each Saturday to me, make a confession, and then listen to a few words of advice, receive a recommendation and some encouragement, and perhaps (but rarely) answer some questions, and then go away with absolution and a penance that usually would be more personal and more fitting to this individual striving to live generously the life of grace. At that time, it was not always encouraged to have individuals come to the rectory office or parlor for individual direction outside the reception of the Sacrament of Penance, especially since the majority of those seeking direction were women.

Personally, I did not fully appreciate the system. While I had no solutions, I still did not experience the satisfaction that the contemporary manner of spiritual direction was the correct and proper one. While I went to confession faithfully (and I am presently using the word confession deliberately because it fits so properly into the pre-Vatican II era), I did not have either a regular confessor or a regular spiritual director. Retreat time at Auriesville with the Jesuit Fathers was usually my time each year for whatever spiritual direction I felt inspired to seek.

I was haunted by words attributed to Saint Bernard and used (as I recall) at a seminary retreat: "He who directs himself is directed by a fool." I was also disturbed mathematically by the thousands of priests and sisters and religious seeking thousands of priests to serve as their spiritual directors. In those days, I never dreamed of being directed by anyone other than a priest. The mere numerical situation made me throw up both hands as if to say: "Something is wrong! There must be a solution."

Finally I gave up. I made it known that I did not consider myself a good choice for spiritual directing. In those days, to be a spiritual director meant (usually), that you were her or his spiritual director for life—or until the Bishop transferred you to another parish a hundred miles away. It was never stipulated for six months or until the New Year or until final profession. It was an on-going commitment usually for better or for worse.

More recently, with the demise of the title, "confession," and with the change over to the Sacrament of Penance or the Sacrament of Reconciliation with its less frequent approach, together with the new thinking created by the Vatican Council, and (strange as it may seem) with the opening up of our rectories and the creation of the reconciliation room, a new birth was given to spiritual direction.

I do not remember for certain who said this to me for the first time, or if I read it in a new publication, nor do I remember the date or circumstance, but I do remember the revelation came as a beautiful, liberating truth that made me want to cry out: "Oh, why didn't someone tell me this before!"

The revelation (at least to me it was a revelation) was: "Our Spiritual Director is Jesus!" His Mother told us that two thousand years ago when she said, "Do whatever he tells you!"

How liberating! How consoling! How available! How beautiful!

Before exploring the many advantages of looking to our Lord as our personal Spiritual Director, it surely will be helpful to consider spiritual direction as it is found in these marvelous years of post Vatican II.

Today, spiritual direction is a revitalized ministry. I wish to introduce you to the Rev. Kevin G. Culligan, O.C.D. who edited (with introductions) a collection of contemporary readings on spiritual direction. In the preface of his book, "Spiritual Direction," Father writes:

"Twenty years ago, I thought spiritual direction was obsolete. It seemed out of touch with modern life...As a ministry in the Church, spiritual direction appeared to have no future. Then came Vatican II...Today many competent spiritual directors respond to the demand for guidance, new training programs prepare directors for the future, and the literature on spiritual direction grows steadily...By presenting readings from reliable authors, also practitioners in the field, I hope to acquaint you with current thinking, practices, and issues in spiritual direction." (Living Flame Press, Box 74, Locust Valley, N. Y. 11560)

I wish to introduce you also to the Rev. William J. Connolly, S.J. and the Rev. William A. Barry, S.J. who wrote "The Practice of Spiritual Direction" (The Seabury Press). In the preface, a very interesting history is given of which here is a brief introduction:

"This book has a history of its own. In 1970 the authors (Father Connolly and Father Barry), with four other Jesuits, began discussing the possibility of starting a spirituality center in the Boston area...In 1971 we six Jesuits founded the 'Center for Religious Development' in Cambridge, Massachusetts, a center whose threefold purpose is:

1. "To do research that contributes to the development of a modern spirituality,
2. "To train experienced men and women for a more effective ministry of spiritual direction, and
3. "To provide spiritual direction to the people of God...

"Over the years our spiritual direction has come to be focused more and more on helping people develop their relationship with God."

My purpose here is only to prove that this ministry has most certainly been revitalized, and to present a few of the names of those who have been pioneers in bringing this about. Let me assure you that there are many others who have pioneered in this ministry, and as you pursue this study of spiritual direction, you will have the honor of meeting them, knowing them and learning from them.

There are many who experience the need to have someone be the channel through which our Lord will direct them in the many events of the spiritual life. While they recognize that Christ is the ultimate Director, they feel called to have Him speak to them through another, a spiritual director, whom they can see and hear and with whom they can talk and share.

It is a consolation to realize that the students of this special ministry have spread out in many directions and are most willing to act as spiritual directors. No longer are such directors limited to priests. Today competent directors are also sisters, brothers, religious, men and women of the laity, married and single. But perhaps in your community, set in a rural area, there is no one except the pastor, a kindly man who always wants to help whenever he can. After talking with you, he truly wants to try to do the very best he can and offers his services in spiritual direction.

Before making a final commitment, it is highly recommended that you both carefully go over these points, discuss them openly and frankly, and draw up a simple plan and schedule before the first conference.

1. That the sessions consist of spiritual direction and not of counseling, except in special situations. If there is a problem of drugs, drinking, unfaithfulness, etc., then counseling is needed. If there is an inner desire to live more fully the life of grace, then spiritual direction is in order.

2. A spiritual mentor gives a direction. Once that direction is established and accepted, spiritual direction is no longer needed. Jesus takes over. Therefore a definite period of time needs to be fixed. For example, the agreement may call for twelve sessions, twice each month for six months, or beginning in Lent, one session each month until the end of the year. At the close of the period, there can be an evaluation of the growth or failure of growth. Even if another series of sessions is suggested, let there be but one more, and that only after a rest period.

3. The session should be conducted in a truly professional manner, that is, without the so called niceties of an afternoon visit. Omit the tea and cakes, the soft background music, and the endless pleasantries. This is serious business and should be treated as such.

4. The length of each session should be mathematically set before the series begins, at least the maximum: usually sixty minutes.

5. These points are never to be trusted to memory. Rather, a copy for the director and a copy for the directee are to be prepared and reviewed from time to time.

6. Ever keep in mind that spiritual direction and the Sacrament of Reconciliation are two different operations. One does not require the other. If the directee desires to receive the Sacrament, it is suggested that the time and the place be distinct from the time and the place of the spiritual direction.

7. Let the directee be open and honest especially in these areas:

    a. What is the directee praying about: Scripture, Ignation Exercises, etc.?
    b. How does the Lord seem to be leading the directee?
    c. How does the directee feel about or experience the life of grace?
    d. How faithful was the directee to the daily practice of prayer?

8. Let the director be open and honest also. Some areas of concern for the director are:

    a. The difficulties of most directees to be open and honest with another.
    b. The importance of asking:
       1) What are you praying about?
       2) How is the prayer going along?
       3) How faithful were you in praying?
       4) How do you feel during your prayer sessions?
    c. The importance of listening much, both sincerely and meaningfully.
    d. The importance of talking little, suggesting little, directing little.
    e. What does our Lord seem to say or suggest or direct?
    f. At the conclusion, give the directee new material (e.g. Scriptural passages) for the prayer sessions.

9. The director must ever keep in mind that Jesus is the true Spiritual Director. Therefore, he or she tries to steer the directee in that direction. Let questions like these be asked.

— What does Jesus think of this?
— Did you ask Jesus to guide you in that?
— Have you prayed to Jesus to send you the Holy Spirit to enlighten you? Jesus is ever present to the directee. Jesus is ever the Spiritual Director. Let the director remember with humility that he or she is only assisting Jesus and assiting the directee in this ministry for a limited period of time. Eventually, Jesus will continue His role as Spiritual Director without the assistance of the director. Jesus will take over completely as the one permanent Spiritual Director. One must not forget the words of Mary: "Do whatever he tells you."

10. If one or the other in these sessions is usually late, forgetful, tired, bored, hurried, confused etc., then let the sessions terminate with kindness. Also, if one or the other seems to be changing his or her role, so that one seems to be taking on the function of the other, terminate the sessions with kindness. (Strange as this may seem, it can easily happen, and in fact does happen more frequently than a person may realize.) If the directee cannot open up or never has anything to say, then again, let the sessions close. If the director merely gives a sermon on a spiritual subject or reads a chapter from a spiritual book, then let the sessions terminate, but always with kidness and gratitude. If the directee is too busy to pray daily, then spiritual direction is impossible.

There are many noble people who are most anxious to serve the Lord and who are most anxious to grow in the life of grace, but there is no one to serve as their spiritual director. What do they do?

The answer is simple. Go to Jesus. Obey Our Lady and do whatever He tells you. She is the Queen of the Saints not only because

she is the Immaculate Conception but also because she practiced what she preached: she went to Jesus for some thirty-three
years and she did whatever He told her. She responded to this
communication lovingly in her own motherly way. What Jesus
shared with Mary had nothing to do with obedience. What Jesus
shared with Mary had to do with love, a life of love, the way
of divine love, a sharing of love. Jesus taught Mary how to have
love on earth, that is, how to have heaven on earth.

How do we today in a world that is drifting farther and farther
away from heaven, knock at the doors of heaven and ask: "Jesus,
what do You want me to do? Jesus, how can I do whatever You
tell me? How can I, like Your mother, do whatever You tell me?"

Here are ways, means and suggestions.

1. Dedicate fifteen minutes (or more) daily to this cause. Let
those fifteen minutes (or more) be taken from primary time. This
cause is too important to be relegated to secondary time, that
is, to time that is used for some other purpose. Never permit
this dedicated time to be obliterated by such meaningless phrases
as:

I haven't got time! or I'm too busy!

2. Honor Jesus with His new title. Say to Him: "Jesus, You are
my Director. Jesus, You are my Spiritual Director. Director Jesus,
guide me and show me the direction. Tell me what to do and
give me the wisdom and the strength to do it...in this
case...and in that case...in this situation...and in that...in
dryness...and in consolation..."

3. In the Gospel according to Saint John, chapter 15, Jesus says
to you and to me:

"You are my friends!...
"I call you friends!...
"I commissioned you to go out and bear fruit,
"fruit that will last."

Therefore, talk to Jesus as you talk to a friend. "Jesus, you are not only my Director, you are my Friend. You and I are friends. As my Friend help me. Guide me. Set me in the right direction. Tell me what to do. My job. . .I hate it. Yet, the salary is good. Should I change jobs? Should I seek a job I like? Can I take the risk and walk out? Will my present job wear me down? I tell You that I shall do whatever You tell me." Talk openly and honestly and sincerely to Jesus. Talk in your own language. Talk in your own manner. But talk to Him. He is your Spiritual Director.

4. Then listen. Waste time listening. When two people share, there is much wasting of time. Between the sharings there are periods of silence. Periods of silence enhance the talking. That is, they frame the talking and make it more meaningful. So listen. . .and listen. . .and listen. . .even listen to nothing. Your willingness to listen (even to nothing) gives honor and glory to God. How often God must want us to keep quiet! How many prayers go rattling into His divine ears and how often He must long for the prayer of silence. . .like the mighty rocks which by just being in existence give Him glory. So listen. . .

5. How simple are the prayers of the Psalms. Psalm 48 says: It is he who leads us!

Read carefully the simple petitions of Psalm 119:

> Bless your servant. Open my eyes that I may see. Show me your commands. Relieve me from scorn and contempt.

Also pray carefully the simple petitions of Psalm 25:

> I trust you; let me not be disappointed. Make me know your way. Lord, teach me your paths. Make me walk in your truth. Teach me. Remember your mercy, Lord. Do not remember the sins of my youth. In your love remember me. Lord, forgive my guilt for it is great. Turn to me and have mercy. Relieve the anguish of my heart. Set me free from my distress. Rescue me. Do not disappoint me.

That is the way to pray. That is the way to talk out to a friend. That is the way to approach one's director. that is the way...

6. Does God always give an answer? Yes, God has three answers. They are:

    a. Yes!
    b. No!
    c. Wait!

7. God has many languages. God communicates with us in many languages. God seldom uses English. God seldom speaks into the ear. God is too creative to use just the ordinary way of communicating. God uses the whole world and all the wonders of the world for His communications...and also He uses all the little things around us. This is a tiny list of some of God's many languages or ways of communication:

> He speaks through sermons. He speaks through grandparents. He speaks through Holy Scripture. He speaks through some special message. He speaks through little children. He speaks through a storm...or a rain drop. He speaks through dreams. He speaks through melodies. He speaks through mothers and fathers and brothers and sisters. He speaks through joys: big ones and little ones. He speaks through friends...and enemies. He speaks through silence. He speaks through snow flakes...and everything.

The story is told of a father who was thinking of moving to the west to take on a new job. But he was not certain. He was confused. What would be best? He prayed. Finally, he said: "Lord, in Your mercy, please give me a sign!" As he was walking home from work, his little boy of six ran out to greet him with a big hug and kiss. "Daddy," said the little fellow looking up at his father, "I love my teacher and I love my new friends in school and I think that they love me. Daddy, please do not ever move us away from here. Please?" With three small tears and with a tiny choke in his throat, the father stopped, squatted down

to his son's level and whispered: "Never!" Then he looked up
to heaven and smiled: "Thank you, Lord!"

That is spiritual direction. That is what Our Lady meant by the
words: "Do whatever he tells you."

8. Does Jesus truly want to help us? Here are His own words.
They mean exactly what they say:

> *"Whoever comes to me, I shall not turn him away."*
> *(John* 6:37).

There is a special quotation from God the Father Who proclaims:

> *"This is my Son, my beloved. Listen to him."* (*Mark*
> 9:7).

Meditate the following quotations. Contemplate these quotations.
That is, hold them in your heart and rest quietly with their meaning as they inspire your heart to great love. Be like the lover
who receives a letter from the one he loves. He holds the letter
over his heart and the message stirs his heart to great love. He
contemplates the letter with its contents as I ask you to contemplate these quotations with their message of deep love.

   a. *"Stand with confidence before the Son of Man."*
      (*Luke* 18:27).
   b. *"Things that are impossible for men are possible
      for God."* (*Luke* 18:27).
   c. *"Ask, and it will be given to you; search, and you
      will find; knock, and the door will be opened to
      you. For the one who asks always receives; the one
      who searches always finds; the one who knocks
      will always have the door opened to him."* (*Luke*
      11:9-10).
   d. *"Courage, your faith has restored you to health."*
      (*Matt.* 9:22).
   e. *"The Son of Man came not to be served but to
      serve."* (*Matt.* 28:20).

f. A woman suffering from hemorrhage only just touched Jesus and He said: *"Somebody touched me. I felt that power had gone out from me."* If only a touch brought forth power, how much more will a strong prayer bring forth power from the merciful heart of Jesus. (*Luke* 8:46).

g. *"If you ask for anything in my name, I will do it."* (*John* 14:14).

h. *"Know that I am with you always."* (*Matt.* 28:20).

If in our lives we are most anxious to serve the Lord and to grow in the life of grace, and if there is no one to serve as our spiritual director, then we go to Jesus. It is that simple. We go to the Lord. We talk. We listen. We follow. This is the Biblical way. This is the way of the early Church. How often Saint Paul was directed to go here but not there, to go this way but not that way. Direction from heaven is available even for us in this sophisticated century in which we live.

To the suggestions already given, I wish to add one last suggestion for those having difficulty in finding spiritual direction. This is not spiritual direction as such, but this is help. . .and there are those who want only a little help now and then.

The suggestion is this: talk things over with a friend. Make no commitment. Do not make your conversation a big deal. Just talk things over. We talk over in friendly, simple, homey, folksy ways the endless list of topics of every day life: the stock market, my job, baseball and football, Washington, the election, a friend who died, the church festival, and on and on. . .Today, it is most acceptable and proper to talk over matters of religion, spiritual things, and one's own spiritual difficulties and desires. For example:

"Bob, let's have lunch tomorrow noon. I need to talk with you. I'm having a difficulty in fulfilling the role of a lector. I need to talk. . ."

"Jim, I've been invited to make a retreat. I've never made one. I understand you go every year. Could I get together with you some night and go over this retreat business with you? I need some help. I think I need to talk..."

"Bill, did you ever read the Bible? I was just given a Bible. I know I should but I really do not know how to use a Bible. Got any ideas...?"

Here are others with whom you can talk things over pertaining to religious or spiritual matters.

Wife with husband and husband with wife!

After the Prayer Group or the Contemplation Group comes to a close, invite one of the participants to stop in with you for a snack and then talk.

Make an appointment with your pastor or with his associate or with the pastoral assistant or the director of religious education in your parish. They are far more anxious to converse with you than you will ever be to converse with them. If there is a deacon in your area or parish, surely you can always call on him. These individuals will look upon your invitation as an honor. They recognize that you are no authority in spiritual matters and they recognize that this is the very reason you are asking to be rescued by them. Phone one of them this week.

If you feel more comfortable, visit the rectory of another parish, or drive out to the retreat house, or phone a relative who is a religious.

The secret is: Do something!

One of the saddest words in the English language is the word "procrastination." (It even sounds sad when it is pronounced.) The word comes from the Latin: to put off until the morrow. The good Lord has been deprived of much honor and glory because of the word procrastination. There is no area in which the word 'act' is as important as in the area of spiritual growth. Again, the secret is: Do something! Act! Now! Immediately! And do not permit procrastination to tempt you to haul out those two stupid American excuses:

I haven't got time! or I'm too busy!

The Bible speaks very wisely of friendships. Friendships are not as popular as they used to be. More and more individuals are going through life without close friends. Friendships need to be cultivated. They do not grow and abound like weeds. I encourage you with all my heart to nourish spiritual friendships in your life and to set aside areas of time in which you can meet and share and grow, knowing that when you are together, the dear Lord is ever in your midst. Holy Scripture cannot help but inspire us to cultivate friendships.

This chapter and also the previous chapters have introduced the reader to many facts. . . maybe too many. The importance of sharing these facts with others cannot be overstressed. These chapters are meant to lead the reader to greater sharing and to more extensive reading.

This particular chapter stresses the sharing element. Spiritual direction, regardless of the method used, is always a form of sharing. Also, the building up of a spiritual library is always a guarantee of expanding one's reading experiences. In growing in the life of Christ, may both sharing and reading ever be fully appreciated and faithfully nourished.

AMEN

This book, PRIMER OF PRAYER, and the following titles dealing with prayer are available from the Riehle Foundation:

PRAY—A MINI COURSE IN SPIRITUALITY
By Rev. Bartholomew O'Brien, 32 pgs. $ .50

THE GOLD BOOK OF PRAYERS
By The Riehle Foundation, 96 pgs. $3.00

THE POWER OF THE ROSARY
By Rev. Albert Shamon, 44 pgs. $2.00

WHY PRAYER? AND HOW TO PRAY
By Rev. René Laurentin, 96 pgs. $4.00

OUR LADY TEACHES ABOUT PRAYER
By Rev. Albert Shamon, 64 pgs. $1.00

The RIEHLE FOUNDATION is a non-profit, tax-exempt publisher and distributor of Catholic books and materials, and also distributes books for Faith Publishing Company. Donations for books, though not required, are appreciated. Suggested values are indicated above. Write to:

THE RIEHLE FOUNDATION
P. O. BOX 7
MILFORD, OHIO 45150

Faith
Publishing
Company

Faith Publishing Company has been organized as a service for the publishing and distribution of materials that reflect Christian values, and in particular the teachings of the Catholic Church.

It is dedicated to publication of only those materials that reflect such values.

Faith Publishing Company also publishes books for The Riehle Foundation. The Foundation is a non-profit, tax-exempt producer and distributor of Catholic books and materials worldwide, and also supplies hospital and prison ministries, churches and mission organizations.

For more information on the publications of Faith Publishing Company, contact:

Faith
Publishing Company
P.O. BOX 237
MILFORD, OHIO 45150